A Year of Tropical Birdsong

First published in the United Kingdom
in 2025 by
Batsford
43 Great Ormond Street
London WC1N 3HZ

An imprint of B.T. Batsford Holdings Ltd

Copyright © B.T. Batsford Ltd, 2025
Text copyright © Dominic Couzens 2025
Illustration copyright © Madeleine Floyd 2025

All rights reserved. No part of this publication may be copied, displayed, extracted, reproduced, utilized, stored in a retrieval system or transmitted in any form or by any means, electronic, mechanical or otherwise including, but not limited to, photocopying, recording, or scanning without the prior written permission of the publishers.

ISBN 978 1 84994 842 5

A CIP catalogue record for this book is available from the British Library.

10 9 8 7 6 5 4 3 2 1

Printed by Toppan Leefung Printing International Ltd, China
Reproduction by Rival Colour Ltd, UK

This book can be ordered direct from the publisher at www.batsfordbooks.com, or try your local bookshop.

A Year
of Tropical
Birdsong

Dominic Couzens

BATSFORD

Contents

WEEK 1	Galápagos penguin	12
WEEK 2	Ocellated antbird	16
WEEK 3	Purple-crested turaco	20
WEEK 4	Fiery-throated hummingbird	24
WEEK 5	Lesser flamingo	28
WEEK 6	Pink pigeon	32
WEEK 7	Blue-and-yellow macaw	36
WEEK 8	King of Saxony bird-of-paradise	40
WEEK 9	Red-capped manakin	44
WEEK 10	Resplendent quetzal	48
WEEK 11	Superb starling	52
WEEK 12	Screaming piha	56
WEEK 13	Black-faced solitaire	60
WEEK 14	Brown wood-owl	64
WEEK 15	Fire-tailed sunbird	68
WEEK 16	Northern carmine bee-eater	72
WEEK 17	Purple-crowned fairywren	76
WEEK 18	Red-billed oxpecker	80
WEEK 19	Oilbird	84
WEEK 20	Indian cuckoo	88
WEEK 21	Eastern paradise-whydah	92
WEEK 22	Blue whistling-thrush	96
WEEK 23	Hooded pitohui	100

WEEK 24	Asian koel	104
WEEK 25	Malayan banded pitta	108
WEEK 26	Bluish-fronted jacamar	112
WEEK 27	Indian peafowl	116
WEEK 28	Dark-necked tailorbird	120
WEEK 29	Black-naped oriole	124
WEEK 30	House crow	128
WEEK 31	Red-headed lovebird	132
WEEK 32	Tiwi	136
WEEK 33	Sparkling violetear	140
WEEK 34	Yellow-crowned gonolek	144
WEEK 35	Golden bowerbird	148
WEEK 36	Bay wren	152
WEEK 37	Rhinoceros hornbill	156
WEEK 38	Red-cheeked cordonbleu	160
WEEK 39	Andean cock-of-the-rock	164
WEEK 40	Common hill myna	168
WEEK 41	Yellow-vented bulbul	172
WEEK 42	Greater bird-of-paradise	176
WEEK 43	Village weaver	180
WEEK 44	Jungle babbler	184
WEEK 45	White-browed robin-chat	188
WEEK 46	Toco toucan	192
WEEK 47	Wompoo fruit-dove	196
WEEK 48	Common potoo	200
WEEK 49	Buff-breasted paradise kingfisher	204
WEEK 50	Harpy eagle	208
WEEK 51	Grey parrot	212
WEEK 52	Tinkling cisticola	216

Introduction

WELCOME TO THE WORLD OF TROPICAL BIRDS AND their songs.
You might well have an idea of what a 'tropical' bird sounds like in your imagination. Perhaps it's a squawk, or a chatter, or something more melodious. In this book you have the sounds at your fingertips, on the page and through the QR codes.

This book introduces 52 tropical species, one for every week of the year. Bird song in the tropics is different to temperate bird song, in that it is much less seasonal, in line with the tropical environment, which lacks the defined winter, spring, summer and autumn (fall) further north or south. Many of the species found in this book vocalize all year round. However, I have tried to choose suitable weeks for each species, tending to choose its peak singing season, if it has one, which is often during the rains.

Hopefully, all your tropical favourites are here. On these pages, you will meet parrots, hummingbirds, toucans, birds-of-paradise, sunbirds, quetzals and many others. Many are dazzling in colouration and the rest are dazzling in their amazing lifestyles, which are often extreme and sometimes strange. Within these pages the QR codes will allow you to hear everything from a macaw's screech to the ethereal loveliness of the black-faced solitaire. Hopefully, a combination of astonishing lifestyle and curious sounds will keep you entertained!

For clarity, it seems sensible to define the tropics and the birds therein. The tropics is the zone between the Tropic of Cancer at about 23°N and the Tropic of Capricorn at 23°S, which encompasses the Equator in the middle at 0° latitude. The zone includes both land and oceans, and accounts for about 40 per cent of the Earth's land surface. For the purposes of this book, any bird that breeds in the tropics is valid for inclusion.

Most people are aware that the tropical zone holds a greater degree of biodiversity than the rest of the planet; about 75 per cent of all the world's species, be they birds, plants, mammals or anything else, are squeezed into its area. As a general rule, this biodiversity reaches its peak nearest the Equator. Thus, you find astonishing disparities between places – a few hectares of equatorial South American forest may hold as many breeding species of birds as the whole of the North American continent, for example. To tread in these forests is to be nestled in the cradle of biodiversity, and it is an astonishing experience.

Intriguingly, there is no complete agreement as to why this area is so species rich, but there are two main hypotheses. One is that tropical regions are simply hotter, wetter and have high productivity and energy in the system; they lack the climatic extremes of north and south, so more species evolve and those that are there are able to survive for longer. The second hypothesis is that there has been more isolation and fragmentation in tropical regions over geological time, for multiple reasons, driving the divergence between species, and this has fostered the extraordinary biodiversity. Whatever the reason, recent studies have found that tropical birds, compared to their northern or southern counterparts, exhibit a wider genetic variation within species, and this variation is more persistent between generations.

There are four main tropical regions with different bird faunas. The New World tropics (neotropics) cover Central and South America and is the richest zone in terms of species; the Afro-tropics cover the African continent; the Asian tropics include much of south-east Asia and nearby islands, but the large island of New Guinea and continental land mass of Australia, plus the various islands of Oceania, is a separate region ornithologically, the Australo-Papuan tropics. For this book, I have chosen about the same number of species from each region.

There are some intriguing differences between temperate and tropical birds, not all of which are understood. One difference that has long been assumed as fact by most people, although based on anecdotal evidence, is that tropical birds are more colourful than the rest. Only recently has this been confirmed by mathematical colour analysis. It found that tropical birds were 30 per cent more colourful than the rest, especially in bright blues and greens, and that the colours were both more varied and more intense. Again, this is likely to be related to the overall energy and resource richness of the tropical ecosystems. If food is more readily available, a bird has more opportunity to put energy into evolving bright colours.

This also works for some of the elaborate displays and breeding behaviour exhibited by tropical birds. It has long been postulated that a diet of fruit, which can be found all year round and requires rather less time to satisfy a bird's daily feeding requirements, has emancipated some male birds from the daily foraging grind and enabled them to evolve sexual ornaments and display routines of quite marvellous splendour. The manakins (see page 44), cotingas (see page 56) and birds-of-paradise (see pages 40 and 176) are all good examples of this, providing the watcher with some of the most exciting wildlife viewing of any on the planet – and usually with a remarkable soundtrack, too. Some individuals may display every day of the year. When displaying against other males, in a communal display called a lek, they are easily compared and contrasted by visiting females, saving the latter the trouble of comparing widely-spaced individuals.

Another breeding system often adopted by tropical birds is group living. Also seen in birds of arid zones, it involves extended families contributing to a communal breeding attempt. One of the factors that enables this to occur is that, at least among songbirds, individuals live longer in the tropics. That means that a young bird can spend a season helping its parents with a new breeding attempt, 'assuming' it will live long enough eventually to graduate to a breeding attempt of its own in future years. Several species in this book, including the purple-crowned fairywren (see page 76), jungle babbler (page 184) and superb starling (page 52) follow this type of lifestyle.

There are several other interesting differences in tropical bird biology, and these are still being studied in an attempt to explain them. For example, temperate birds lay consistently larger clutches of eggs: in an analysis of 5,000 species, tropical birds laid two eggs on average and temperate birds 4.5 eggs. However, in another study, it seems that tropical birds try more clutches per year. In yet another study, it was discovered that tropical songbirds grow their wings more quickly than temperate birds, meaning that they fly well when they fledge. It is thought that, with such diversity in the forests generally, there are more potential predators, so learning to fly as soon as possible is a good survival strategy. The upshot, though, is that tropical parents feed their chicks for longer than temperate birds, because the chicks' overall weight increases more slowly in the tropics.

And, of course, songs and other vocalisations also show differences. As mentioned above, one is that tropical bird songs are much less seasonal. Singing effort may increase prior to and during the rains, when a bird is preparing for breeding, but it many cases it continues all year round.

A reminder is in order here that there is a broad distinction used everywhere between bird SONGS and bird CALLS. SONGS are the typically complex vocalisations that birds use to make a point – perhaps defend a territory or attract a mate, or both. Songs also stimulate birds' brains to release hormones associated with breeding, and typically help a male and female to be synchronized physiologically. CALLS are simpler vocalisations, often just a single note or two, that are used in multiple situations, such as contact or alarm. In the tropics, members of mixed parties tend just to give calls to keep together. Call notes may not be associated directly with breeding, but songs always are.

That said, one very significant difference between the tropics and temperate zones is that female song is much more significant and frequent in the former. There are a small number of species in which females sing more than males (such as the streak-backed oriole of Central America and Mexico in parts of its range) and, since this is an area where research is quite intensive, there will no doubt be many more discovered. But generally speaking, it is very common in the tropics for females to sing loudly and frequently, whereas it is unusual in temperate areas.

There are probably several reasons for this. In the tropics, songbirds live longer and often form long-lasting, stable pair bonds. In this situation, it makes sense that both would contribute to the usual role of song, which is to defend a territory from other birds or pairs. At the same time, in places where seasons are less well-defined and there are fewer cues to begin breeding, if both members of a pair sing they can mutually stimulate each other and prepare in synchrony for breeding.

Related to this is another typically tropical phenomenon, duetting. It isn't exclusive to the tropics, but it is much more common in this region. It is found in about 200 species worldwide, including the bay wren (see page 152) and the yellow-crowned gonolek (see page 144), and will probably be found in many more. Duetting involves the male and female singing at the same time. Sometimes they will simply alternate their contributions (antiphonal duets) but at other times they will integrate in a far more complex and intricate manner – it can be all but impossible, listening, to tell that it is two birds, not one bird, vocalizing. Duets are associated with birds that have long term monogamous pair bonds, and in its simplest form a duet can enable a member of the pair to know that its partner is nearby. Duets can also be aimed at neighbouring pairs and competitors, ensuring that territories and pair bonds are preserved.

This book, therefore, is a celebration of all things to do with tropical birds, from their bright colours to their unusual and complex lifestyles. The soundtrack is as varied as the birds themselves. Hopefully, you will find and hear something that you find inspiring and amazing.

As ever, with any such book, there is a sadness in writing it. No reader will be unaware that tropical birds all around the world face large population declines in line with their shrinking habitat. This book is a reminder that the world is an astonishing place and the wildlife within it has the capacity to thrill us and make our lives immeasurably better. Everything, from the birds themselves to the sounds that they make, is worth preserving.

Dominic Couzens
UK, September 2024

WEEK 1

Galápagos penguin

Spheniscus mendiculus

GALÁPAGOS ISLANDS, OFF WESTERN SOUTH AMERICA

48–53cm (19–21in)

THERE WILL BE PLENTY OF TROPICAL favourites featured in this book, but let's begin with a penguin. After all, what bird would you least expect to find among the parrots and hummingbirds on these pages? Perhaps one that is supposed to live with a backdrop of icebergs? Yet here it is, completely worth its place, a bird that doesn't just live in a very hot climate but occurs right on the Equator, the very heart of the tropics. And, whisper it quietly, it also lives permanently in the Northern Hemisphere, which penguins 'are not supposed to do'.

The Galápagos penguin is still an outlier and owes its existence to the cold-water currents of the Pacific Ocean, two of which, the Humboldt and Cromwell currents, flow as far north as the Galápagos Islands. Despite all the photos you have seen, what penguins really need is not cold land but cold water. Some of the world's most productive oceans, where turbulence is the norm and nutrients are swept violently up towards the water surface, are found in the seas and oceans around Antarctica. But cold currents can also flow north. The waters off the Galápagos are unusually cold and unusually productive, hence the anomaly. Not too far to the south, another penguin, the Humboldt penguin (*S. humboldti*), lives on the coast of Peru. Both are very small species.

In these curious surroundings, penguins still do penguin things. The Galápagos penguin spends much of its time in the water chasing fish, in this case usually no more than 60m (200ft) from the shore. It relies on large shoals of small species such as anchovies, mullet and sardines. It tends to dive below a shoal and snatch them as it heads for the surface. Although we typically think of penguins as fast swimmers, they don't reach speeds more than 2m (6½ft) per second when hunting. At night it roosts on land but spends almost all its day in the water.

For breeding, these penguins don't have very much choice, so they use crevices in the volcanic rocks of the islands where they breed (Fernandina, Isabela). Where there is loose soil, they will dig a burrow. This species breeds twice a year, with a peak in egg laying at this time of year (December to March) and another between June and September, quite a contrast to the larger penguins, which might raise one chick every one and a half years. The normal clutch is two, and the youngsters hatch anywhere between two and four days apart, which usually favours the older nestling. The pair bond is exceptionally stable in this species; 93 per cent of all adults remain together between one year and the next. Divorce is a pretty risky process when your entire population is only 2000 birds.

Galápagos penguins are always vulnerable to the vagaries of the cold currents that are their lifeblood. Whenever the local waters heat up to 25°C (77°F), the populations of fish plummet and breeding success crashes. Every time there is an El Niño event, the cold current is reduced in strength and the penguins either try to breed and quickly fail, or they don't try to breed at all. Unfortunately, these events are becoming increasingly common, with the seas being too warm too often. This delightful penguin is already listed as Endangered on the IUCN Red List of Threatened Species, and its future is in very real peril.

The Galápagos penguin spends much of its time in the water chasing fish, in this case usually no more than 60m (200ft) from the shore.

For now, though, the Galápagos penguin continues to defy our perceptions of its family, and here's an astonishing thought. On the Galápagos Islands, penguins may incubate their eggs in extreme heat, sometimes as high as 40°C (104°F). Contrast this with their relatives in the same family, the Emperor penguins (*Aptenodytes forsteri*), which incubate eggs on their feet at ambient Antarctic temperatures of -40°C (-40°F). That's a remarkable range within a single bird family.

WEEK 2

Ocellated antbird

Phaenostictus mcleannani

CENTRAL AND NORTHERN SOUTH AMERICA

17–20cm (6¾–8in)

 IT'S DAYBREAK IN A LOWLAND RAINFOREST in Central America. Out of the darkness comes a loud, accelerating, then decelerating whistle, vaguely recalling a blast from a sports referee. This is the song of the ocellated antbird, and it's a bird in a hurry. It's the antbirds' rush hour.

Trying to locate an ocellated antbird in the morning gloaming can be a fool's game. You might hear one close by and peer into the understorey hopefully, but the chances are that it will move on rapidly before you spot it. The next song may be from around a corner on the forest trail, then the next a little further away. This is because, unlike most birds singing in the forest at dawn, this one is on the move.

The reason for the antbird's skittish daybreak behaviour is that it is searching for the right place to begin its foraging for the day. It's not looking for a glade of sunlight or a fruiting tree, but something much more unusual. It is searching for a moving column of soldier ants (*Eciton* spp.).

The primary rainforests of the neotropics play host to huge colonies of these formidable insects. These are the ones that sweep across the forest floor, catching and killing every invertebrate (or small vertebrate) in their path. In a raid lasting a day, 200,000 marching ants may kill up to 100,000 other animals; the next day is the same. At night the ants make bivouacs out of their own bodies, fitted together using hooks on their feet. But at daybreak, the rivers of ants flow out once again and may be 100m (330ft) long.

It is these columns that the ocellated antbird is seeking. You might quickly assume that the ants themselves are nourishment for the birds, but this isn't the case. Instead, the birds station themselves at the margins of the columns, particularly at the front, because what they are after are the invertebrates fleeing the ants. Knowing that doom awaits them if they stay still, many thousands of insects, spiders and others flee for

The ocellated antbird is unusual for being what is known as an obligate ant-follower: it spends its entire life following ants and never feeds anywhere else.

their lives; it is at this moment of vulnerability that the antbirds strike. It might be a kinder death. Most animals that the ocellated antbird eats are smaller than 25mm (1in) in length.

Effectively, then, the antbirds are cashing in on the ants' raids, and they aren't the only ones. Within these superabundant forests there is a whole guild of species that do the same thing; these aren't just antbirds, but birds from many other families as well. At the swarm there is a hierarchy. The ocellated antbird, being larger than most, is dominant, and often forces other birds away from the best perches at the head of the ant column. The ant followers often stay around 2m (6½ft) above ground, and are especially adept at clinging on to vertical stems.

Within the ant-following guild, there are differing levels of dedication. Some species come and go, alternating the odd bout of ant-following with other, more conventional types of foraging. Some species are only occasional followers. But the ocellated antbird is unusual for being what is known as an obligate ant-follower: it spends its entire life following ants and never feeds anywhere else. Even when attending its nest during breeding, it still visits the ant columns. Only in the stable and extraordinarily rich and diverse habitat of a tropical forest could such specialization occur.

Ocellated antbirds have quite large territories of about 50ha (124 acres). Within this territory, multiple ant colonies occur and a given pair will visit a number of these each day. Their most important appointment, though, is in the early morning, and the first meal of the day.

WEEK 3

Purple-crested turaco

Gallirex porphyreolophus

SOUTHERN EAST AFRICA

42–46cm (16½–18in)

TURACOS ARE THE PUBLIC ADDRESS systems of African forests. Every daybreak, groups of these birds announce the dawn with loud barking calls. When one group proclaims from the dimly lit treetops, the neighbouring group is stimulated to do the same, and so their crowing resonates through the district as everyone awakes. Local legend has it that turacos call on the hour, every hour, and nearby farmers can time their activities accordingly. There are more melodic birds that welcome the African dawn, but the turacos are the loudest. It is almost as if they have heard about the famous sound of that other herald of the dawn – the cockerel – and this is their attempt to emulate it.

The purple-crested turaco, found in evergreen and riverine forests in the south-east segment of tropical Africa, has one of the more elaborate reveilles among its small family of 24 species, often emitting 10–15 or more grating calls in sequence. In common with many members of the family, hearing it is a lot easier than catching a glimpse. Turacos are the very definition of an arboreal bird, spending almost all their time in the forest canopy and this means that, despite their size, they can be difficult to spot. The best time is when a pair or group decide to move trees; they tend to do this in single file, each bird flapping at treetop height, slightly unsteadily, the long tail trailing behind.

For many centuries, turaco feathers have been much prized and placed in head-dresses.

The feet of turacos are unusual. They have four toes, two facing forward and two back, but one of the back toes can rotate almost 70 degrees, allowing remarkable flexibility when the bird is in the tree canopy, where it may need to run along branches or hang in awkward positions. Turacos are more agile in the trees than they are in the air.

What they are seeking in the forest canopy is fruit, their exclusive diet. In common with many tropical birds, they are particularly fond of figs, but they eat a very wide range and have been recorded eating 134g (4¾ oz) of food in a day. Most of the fruits are swallowed whole.

This frugivorous diet has a curious ramification. Many of the fruits concerned contain small amounts of copper, and this has enabled the turacos to evolve unusual copper-based pigments that suffuse their plumage. Most members of the family are highly coloured birds, with shimmering green on the body, often with iridescence, showy crests and flashes of red in the wing. Scientists have found that the red colour comes from a pigment known as turacin, and the green is from a compound called turacoverdin. Astonishingly, neither of these pigments are found anywhere else in the Animal Kingdom – and they aren't even found on all turacos. Several bush country species are just dull and grey.

It's been calculated that the red plumage of a single turaco can yield 8 milligrams of copper and that, in order to keep their plumage colourful, individuals must eat 20kg (44lb) of fruit over a three-month period. There is a rather charming – but quite wrong and somewhat persistent – legend that it only takes a shower of heavy rain to wash the shiny green plumage off. The fact that turacos are inveterate bathers, and often spend long minutes in puddles, disproves the theory.

As well as being noisy and bright, turacos are common throughout sub-Saharan Africa so it's no surprise that they are a part of the culture of forest peoples. For many centuries, turaco feathers have been much prized and placed in head-dresses, the red colouration being particularly significant, and viewed as high ranking. Bearing in mind the remarkable and unique pigments on display, these status symbols become all the more significant for this.

WEEK 4

Fiery-throated hummingbird

Panterpe insignis

CENTRAL AMERICA

10–11cm (4–4½in)

WHO DOESN'T LOVE HUMMINGBIRDS? FEW birds have their charisma or glittering colours. They include most of the world's smallest birds (including the smallest, the bee hummingbird (*Mellisuga helenae*), at just 5–6cm (2–2¼in) long), but few make a bigger impression. Nobody ever forgets their first hummingbird. Their popularity is reflected in the fact that, through the neotropics, thousands of lodges, hotels and even restaurants have hummingbird feeders to attract guests. Nobody ever tires of watching them.

At such feeders, while you might be enchanted by their extraordinary powers of flight, you might also notice that, while they might be shrunk, they are not shrinking violets. Many are highly aggressive. Skirmishes are constant, fights are common. Whatever colours shimmer within their plumage, they see red.

Lots of hummers are irritable, and a good example is this one, a species from the highlands of Costa Rica and Panama. Watch any feeder in this area and the fiery-throated hummingbird shows off its fiery temper. Usually dominant, it chases off both of its own sub-species (*P. i. insignis* and *P. i. eisenmanni*) and those of other species, beginning with the loud chittering call you can hear in the recording, and continuing with some in-your-face hovering. It's the same at flowers that are away from artificial sugar feeders. The only thing a male will tolerate in its patch of flowers is a female hummingbird. At this time of year, in the breeding season, males defend these patches of flowers, and allow access to any female that mates with them, a sort of sex-for-nectar arrangement. Fiery-throated hummingbirds are generalists, drinking from many different species of flowers, and they don't have any particular affinity with specific blooms, as many hummers do. They also frequently 'cheat' the flowers, by using holes made in the bottom of blooms by other birds and by bees. Nevertheless, they are very important pollinators for a number of rare plants.

The more you watch hummingbirds, the more astonishing they seem. The hovering flight at flower heads is almost unique, although a few sunbirds (Nectariniidae) occasionally do the same for short periods of time. The wingbeat rate of hummers is normally about 70 beats a second, but while chasing or during display this can rocket up to 200 beats a second, which is more than an insect such as a hoverfly. The wings are almost entirely composed of digits of the hand, meaning that these birds fly more or less with their fingers. When hovering, the wingtips make a figure of eight pattern, which is so aerodynamically stable that hummingbirds can fly forwards, backwards and, of course, upside down. To add to their lists of superlatives, they are also among the fastest-flying birds in the world, typically flying at 50–80km (31–50 miles) per hour and touching 95km (60 miles) per hour in bursts.

The amazing flying abilities of hummingbirds are stunning, but perhaps what makes us enjoy them like few other birds are their stunning colours. You use whatever words you like for their jewel-like quality, but you won't do better than the many descriptions used in hummingbird names – glittering, shining, scintillant and many more. Of the 369 currently recognized species, 53 are named after gemstones, but the quality they are all describing in scientific terms is known as iridescence.

The fiery-throated hummingbird is a great example of one with particularly obvious iridescence; the throat would not look "fiery" without it. The curiosity is that the colour is not caused by a pigment at all. Most hummingbirds are not colourful in the typical sense of the word. Instead, everything that we see is what is reflected back at us from the structure of the feathers. And what is amazing about iridescence is that the colour of the light that you see from one angle is different to that seen from another angle. The same feather reflects more than one colour of light, as you can tell as the bird turns its head.

Fiery-throated hummingbirds are generalists, drinking from many different species of flowers.

In order to understand iridescence properly you probably need a degree in physics, but what everyone can grasp is that the light reflected back is controlled by nanostructures of extraordinary complexity and precision. As if hummingbirds weren't exceptional enough, the minutiae of their feathers might just be the biggest wonder of all.

There are nanostructures for nano-birds! How perfect!

WEEK 5

Lesser flamingo

Phoeniconaias minor

LOCALIZED IN AFRICA AND NORTH-WEST INDIA/PAKISTAN

80–90cm (31½–35½in)

THERE ARE FEW MORE SPECTACULAR sights in the warmer parts of the world than a flock of flamingos. The noise they make is less impressive, as you can tell from the recording, a honking quite similar to a goose. However, in the wild, large flocks produce a loud murmur or a roar, depending on how many there are.

Flamingos are unique birds in many ways. They have extraordinary long, bare legs, making them tall (the lesser flamingo stands just under 1m (3¼ft) tall), and they have correspondingly long necks. This is because they customarily bend down to their feet to feed, making them the only birds that almost always feed upside down. The head is small, and the bill is characteristically kinked in the middle. All the species have pink plumage, the carotenoid pigment coming from their diet.

All flamingos live in shallow water with an extremely high alkaline content. Lesser flamingos are virtually the only organism able to survive in certain hypersaline lakes, save for their primary foodstuff – and the reason they are there – which is a blue-green algae from the genus *Spirulina*; a few diatoms also enter the diet. As a result, lesser flamingos have no competitors and few predators. No ground-living animal can survive crossing the treacherous salt flats where the birds breed; intruders could easily become lodged in the mud and die under the sun, with temperatures reaching up to 55°C (131°F) in some areas.

The extremity of the habitat means that lesser flamingos can only breed in a small number of special sites (the larger species have a broader diet and are more widespread). They convene in enormous colonies in these locations. It is fairly routine for colonies to exceed a million pairs, and on Lake Magadi, Kenya, in the 1960s, the number of birds was estimated at 2.4 million – one of the largest breeding aggregations of birds ever recorded. Most lesser flamingos occur on a handful of lakes in east Africa's Rift Valley, although they are also found in south and west Africa, with a few in north-west India and Pakistan. Conditions for breeding, especially water level, have to be exactly right. They don't reproduce every year, and they often switch between sites *en masse*.

Flamingos famously build nests out of mud, far out on these inhospitable lakes.

The flamingo bill is highly specialized for its diet. *Spirulina* species are microscopic and must be filtered out of the water using a very fine mechanism. The lower mandible contains a large central groove and also acts as a flotation device. Meanwhile, the upper mandible is heavily keeled and is deeply and densely grooved, the plates fitting together like those of a baleen whale, another filter feeder. On the plates are hairs that exclude all particles except those that the flamingo wishes to retain, which are in the range of 40–200 micrometres. The two mandibles fit tightly together and the bird uses its tongue as a piston to force water through the hairs and plates. Particles are filtered out and swallowed. If you ever wondered why the flamingo has a bent bill, the answer is simple. In an open straight bill, the critical gap between mandibles is wide at the tip and narrow at the base. With a bent bill, the gap between mandibles is much more constant.

Flamingos famously build nests out of mud, far out on these inhospitable lakes. The overall shape is a cone with a flat top, which reaches 20–40cm (8–15¾in) above the lethal mud, which can be hot enough to kill the chick. The female lays a single egg, and both sexes take it in turn to incubate, sometimes putting in shifts of up to 24 hours. The chick hatches at 28 days and is then fed by regurgitation from both parents. Once on its feet, the youngster joins in enormous créches, which huddle together and move as one. Amazingly, even among a créche of hundreds of thousands of youngsters, the adults hear and recognize the call of their chick as they come to feed it.

On some lakes, if the water levels begin to fall too quickly, the youngsters have to walk as far as 50km (30 miles) to reach permanent pools of water. This is a treacherous trek and many perish along the way, either from starvation or predation by African fish eagles (*Icthyophaga vocifer*) or marabou storks (*Leptoptilos crumenifer*). If they make it through those dangerous early days, flamingos can live for 20–40 years.

WEEK 6

Pink pigeon

Nesoenas mayeri

ISLAND OF MAURITIUS, INDIAN OCEAN

40cm (15¾in)

FORTY YEARS AGO, I SAT ON AN ELEVATED hide in the Black River Gorge in Mauritius, looking over a patch of woodland. It felt like a sacred place, and in some ways, it was. It was certainly secret, with few people being allowed access. At the time (1983), this small grove was the only place on earth with a viable population of one of the rarest birds then in existence, the Mauritius pink pigeon. During a bucolic afternoon, with the tropical sun descending and causing the birds' plumage to glow as pink as the sunset, the privilege of watching these birds was almost tangible. The birds cooed gently like lowing cows.

At the time, the world population was thought to be about 10–20 birds, teetering on the brink of oblivion. I look back on that day with mixed feelings, because it was almost the equivalent of spending time with a dying person – overwhelmingly precious, but profoundly sad.

The pink pigeon is one of many island birds throughout the world that have struggled with human occupation of their only home. Islands are, by nature, confined areas, and island populations, if not low, have nowhere to go to expand. People have a habit of trashing places everywhere they go, and Mauritius has suffered much the same as everywhere else. Forests were cut down, endemic animals were shot for food and, to add to the misery, humankind brought things they needed, such as pigs and goats, and imported plants that took over the habitat from the fragile endemics. People also brought things they didn't need, such as rats, which escaped and ravaged the island with gleeful abandon. Due to such pressures, many of Mauritius's endemics perished.

The pink pigeon, though, proved somewhat less destructible than everyone expected in 1983. It had survived into the 1980s when others hadn't, after all. From that time, the wonderful Carl Jones MBE, a Welsh biologist, took an interest in the pigeon's fate. Through intensive conservation measures, including captive breeding, the population gradually recovered. The birds rely on native vegetation to feed, and through habitat restoration, more of this became available. Several of the pigeon's predators, such as rats and crab-eating macaques (*Macaca fascicularis*) were controlled. The pigeons were given supplementary food. Nests were closely guarded. Broods were manipulated to assure genetic diversity and promote survival of the young. Captive bred birds were reintroduced, including on to an offshore island, Île aux Aigrettes.

It has taken vast resources, time, ingenuity and imagination, and lashings of human love and dedication to save the pink pigeon. Once listed as Critically Endangered on the IUCN Red List, it is now rated Vulnerable. These days, its wild population numbers about 300 birds, with others in captive breeding establishments. In future, additional habitats could be created by planting more native vegetation, and the bird could even be introduced to Mauritius's neighbour, La Réunion, over 200km (124 miles) away, and other nearby islets. The future does look rosy, if not pink.

Of course, you might know of the island's 'other' pigeon, the Mauritius blue pigeon (*Alectroenas nitidissimus*), which was hunted to extinction in the early 19th century. However, you certainly will have heard of the pink pigeon's more famous relative, the dodo (*Raphus cucullatus*), probably the most famous extinct bird in the world. Other than subfossil bones and a few anatomically suspect sketches, staggeringly little is known about this bird – what it ate, how it reproduced or even what it really looked like. It was unprepared to be confronted by human culture; some dodos were taken overseas, but little was learned. Now, all we really know is that they aren't here anymore. The last ones were seen sometime between 1662 and 1693 – we don't even know exactly when.

These days, its wild population numbers about 300 birds, with others in captive breeding establishments.

Oh, to have been on Mauritius 400 years ago, not 40! That would have been an even greater privilege.

WEEK 7

Blue-and-yellow macaw

Ara ararauna

SOUTH AMERICA
76–86cm (30–34in)

SOMEBODY SHOULD CREATE A MOBILE phone ringtone, or better still, an alarm, featuring the screech of a macaw. The segment would have to build up, from gentle conversational calls of a pair to the yells of a flock echoing across the forest. That would definitely get you out of bed.

Seeing a wild macaw is a curious experience. We are so used to seeing these giant parrots in zoos or in adventure films that having the opportunity to admire them in their natural habitat is a delightful jolt. They are magnificent as they commute over the undisturbed forests of Central and South America, in pairs or family parties, with their slow, full, magisterial wingbeats, stately, unhurried pace and princely train of tail feathers trailing behind and their voices echoing all around. They are capable of travelling 100km (62 miles) in a day, seeking out the choicest fruits, nuts, seeds and leaves at their leisure. They perch high up and have an air of superiority, the top-notch top dogs of the treetops.

In western Amazonia in particular, macaws also spend their time seeking out something else entirely, and something quite mysterious and unexpected. Almost every day, they descend to clay licks, or *collpas* – exposed cliffs or raised river banks – in order to eat clay. Known as geophagy, it is highly unusual among birds, and it also looks distinctly strange. The birds land at the cliff, use their mighty bills to extract the soil, and after a few minutes they fly up to the treetops and appear to keep munching away at it with apparent satisfaction. The whole visit is a social occasion. At a single *collpa*, up to 200 macaws of various species may be seen in a single morning, along with 20 more other species of parrots. The lick is clearly an important place, and the clay-chewing is so necessary that the visitors large and small cling to the *collpa* in an exposed position, where predators could potentially reach them.

They are capable of travelling 100km (62 miles) in a day, seeking out the choicest fruits, nuts, seeds and leaves at their leisure.

For many years it was postulated that the birds came to take in neutralizing minerals. Macaws, along with other parrots, eat many plants that are full of toxins, and the theory was that the clay prevented them from being poisoned. However, recent studies have shown that this doesn't work. Instead, it is now thought that the birds come for salt, a vital mineral that is scarce in the Amazon basin. The phenomenon of birds visiting *collpas* is greater in those areas that are furthest from the prevailing wind from the sea (which is from the east). So, it seems that they are essentially visiting a health spa.

Whatever the reason, it is one of the great sights of the Amazon, a part of the world that hardly lacks for natural marvels. To see one blue-and-yellow, scarlet or green-winged macaw is awesome; to see several individuals of all these species, with their power and grace and gaudy colours, all close to each other on a cliff face, is overwhelming.

And, of course, there is the noise. As mentioned above, a macaw volley packs a punch. To hear a whole firing range of croaking shouts, like a convention of sergeant-majors, is like being stuck in the middle of a slanging match between a mob of people you don't know. It is also a way of being immersed into the wilds of Amazonia, the sounds breaking through the bubble of your incredulity.

The macaws visit the licks in the early morning, just as the sun rises and stains the brown cliffs orange. In this part of the world, the macaw alarm clock is genuine.

WEEK 8

King of Saxony bird-of-paradise

Pteridophora alberti

NEW GUINEA

20–22cm (8–8½in)

EVOLUTION THROWS UP SOME REAL LIVING curveballs, and one of those is the male King of Saxony bird-of-paradise. Honestly, if you wanted to dream up a more ridiculous duo of ornaments than two long plumes originating from the bird's ear coverts behind the eyes and draping down more than twice the length of its body, you probably couldn't. And these crazy plumes also look a little bit cheap and nasty, like a blue string of plastic bunting. It's difficult not to recall those snaps you often see of human fashion shows, where a model is wearing something that all the fashionistas wow over, but the rest of the world says, 'Er, no.'

But just to confound you further, what kind of noise is this same bird making, at the same time? How to describe it ... well, it's rather like the static you used to hear on an old-fashioned radio, or very rapid-fire lip-smacking, or maybe the sound of a lawn sprinkler. However you describe it, it's weird. The sight and sound of the King of Saxony is a double whammy of, shall we be kind and say – originality? Let's face it, the Queen of Saxony cannot be a girl who wants to remain mainstream and traditional.

The birds-of-paradise of New Guinea are simply, mindbogglingly marvellous. They make it seem as though one day a crow-like ancestor settled down in its absurdly rich forests and went on to mix natural selection with copious quantities of alcohol. Or maybe something stronger. The result is a range of forms of such opulence and extravagance that it seems that birds, all birds, have collectively decided to give away their most outrageous outfits to the birds-of-paradise. And the King of Saxony got one of the more outlandish.

The purpose of it all, as always, is to impress that potential mate. The male King of Saxony is one of the birds-of-paradise that is thought to display entirely on its own, and lure as many females as possible with its calls and posturing. It isn't fussy, any female will do; the male plays no part in nesting or looking after eggs or young,

The plumes and sounds play an important part, but the male King of Saxony also needs to impress with visual postures.

so it doesn't have to assess the female. The female, on the other hand, simply listens to all the local males and her choice is very important. She needs a good-quality male to ensure that her own offspring will have the best genetic material for life.

The plumes and sounds play an important part, but the male King of Saxony also needs to impress with visual postures, and interestingly, these take two very different forms. First, the male selects a high perch, often in a 'traditional' location that has been used by birds down the years; it is usually in a tall tree emerging above the rest of the canopy. Here, the male calls loudly and, essentially, throws its plumes about. He will thrust them forwards, as if pointing at something, and then extend them both horizontally at a 90-degree angle out from his face. At the same time, he opens his gape wide, revealing the startlingly green interior of his mouth, and ruffles his flanks and back.

If this attracts a female, the male then takes proceedings down into the murky understorey. He then does a lot of similar displaying, but also adds in something very different. He takes hold of a vine and, keeping his grip, bounces up and down rhythmically, by flexing his legs. This will have the effect of swaying all the accompanying vines including, hopefully, the one upon which the watching female is perched. If all goes well, his precopulatory display involves pointing those ever-so-marvellous plumes directly towards her, as if they are giant antennae.

Hence, the birds engage. Natural selection has done its job and evolution takes a celebratory swig.

WEEK 9

Red-capped manakin

Ceratopipra mentalis

CENTRAL AND NORTHERN SOUTH AMERICA

10–11cm (4–4½in)

HERE'S A QUESTION FOR YOU. WHAT IS the connection between an obscure Central American tropical bird and the late megastar musician Michael Jackson? The answer is the moonwalk, a dance move popularized by Jackson to such an extent that it was the title of his autobiography. It is a stunningly clever routine in which the performer motions to go forward but instead slides backwards. Jackson used it in a TV performance to his track 'Billy Jean' in 1983 and it caused a sensation.

It's hardly a new manoeuvre, though: the red-capped manakin has been doing just the same, probably for hundreds of thousands of years. It's part of an elaborate routine this bird uses to impress a visiting female. It's for an audience of one, rather than the millions Jackson enjoyed.

The red-capped manakin's breeding strategy is one that is found in a few tropical birds. The males spend large amounts of time displaying communally, with several males within sight or sound of each other, an arrangement known as a lek. The female visits a lek, or often several leks, in order to assess the quality of the males there, comparing them all. The contribution of the male to the breeding attempt consists of sperm and nothing else; the dull-plumaged, retiring female is responsible for all breeding duties, from nest building to bringing up the young.

Since females only require sperm from the males, they are exceptionally choosy about whom they mate with. Only the best will do, and over years that puts selection pressure on males to come up with ways to display their fitness. In the case of manakins, that is mainly a display, accompanied by sounds.

The devotion of male manakins to their display is extraordinary. Many spend 90 per cent of the day on their display perches at the lek, spending just a few minutes gathering enough fruit to keep themselves alive. And they do this virtually every day of the year. They display even when females are not present, especially in the early hours of the morning, since they are also competing one with another. They make breathy whistles as they do so. When a female does visit, their displaying naturally becomes intense, and every male at the lek is suddenly energized.

Red-capped manakins select a perch that is about 5–15m (16–50ft) above the ground, quite narrow, horizontal and with an unobstructed view of the surrounding area. About five males gather in each lek, spaced between 3m and 30m (10–100ft) apart – so they can't always see one another, but they can always hear.

The display has four components, of which the backward slide is the most extraordinary. The male manakin, which has mostly black plumage, suddenly stretches up to reveal the most striking yellow thighs, as if wearing furry long johns. It bows down, its white eye blazing, and sidles backwards along the perch, with rapid, barely visible steps, often for 5–10cm (2–4in); he might then turn and slide the other way. If a female is present, he slides backwards towards her. It is very hard to observe this in the wild without wanting to burst out laughing.

A different display involves another remarkable manakin feature. Known as the 'about face', it involves the male stretching up to reveal its colourful thighs once again, looking in one direction, and then suddenly switching to look the other way. This involves an exceptionally rapid change of feet, of which any human dancer would be proud, and at the same time, a flap of the wings so rapid that it makes a loud snapping sound. When you are walking through the forest, it is these snaps that alert you to manakin activity.

The males spend large amounts of time displaying communally, with several males within sight or sound of each other, an arrangement known as a lek.

A third component involves simply flying from one perch to another, again wing-snapping. These movements of the wings are so quick that, even if you are watching a manakin through binoculars, it is quite possible to miss them altogether. They sound like the crack of a whip.

The fourth display is a circular flight and, as it lands, it makes a loud 'tearing' sound and stalls on its approach. This is often the culmination of successful courtship. The male quickly mounts the female, and its life's work is done.

WEEK 10

Resplendent quetzal

Pharomachrus mocinno

CENTRAL AMERICA

MALE 90cm (35½in) INCLUDING TAIL, FEMALE 37cm (14½in)

 IF A BIRD APPEARS ON A COUNTRY'S banknotes, it's fair to assume it is a well-known and popular icon. If the local currency is actually named after a bird, then it's obvious that the bird is of immense cultural importance to the area. So is the resplendent quetzal to the country of Guatemala, where you pay for everything in quetzals and their symbol is on the coat of arms and on postage stamps, and is generally ubiquitous.

Yet the country's current idolization of its most fabulous bird is nothing compared to how much it was revered in ancient times, as part of both the Mesoamerican Maya (250–1697) and Aztec (1300–1521) cultures. Quetzal feathers were of untold value to these peoples and demonstrated high worth and luxury. Stone images of quetzals and their feathers abound at their ruins. The Maya used the tail feathers as a medium of exchange, hence their adoption as modern currency. A few Aztec headdresses survive and are notable for the sheer numbers of feathers used, in one case 450 (each bird yields just four long plumes). They were worn by priests, noblemen and especially rulers. The Aztec emperor Moctezuma II is thought to have conquered a neighbouring state simply because of its rich quetzal population, and every year, special merchants were sent out to all corners of the empire to collect these glinting ornaments. It is thought that the trade amounted to more than 6000 feathers a year. However, those collecting the feathers were not allowed to kill the living birds, on pain of death.

The quetzal was thought to be a link between the human and the divine.

More significantly, however, the quetzal was thought to be a link between the human and the divine. Quetzal feathers are iridescent, appearing to be different colours from different angles. An emperor shrouded with the long plumes displayed his exalted humanity, his godlike status. And one of the Aztec deities was Quetzalcoatl, the god of light, life, wisdom and wind, arts and crafts. To these people, the quetzal wasn't just a bird.

The earthly resplendent quetzal is a jewel from the upland forests of Central America, from southern Mexico to western Panama. It mainly occurs between 1000 and 3300m (3300 and 11,000ft), although there is evidence that it may fly to lower altitudes after breeding. It nests in holes in trees and spends much of its time eating fruits, especially avocados. It is somewhat sluggish. As you can tell from the recording, there is nothing particularly special about its advertising call, a repeated 'tok' that sounds rather like the distressed bark of a puppy.

Of course, the quetzals have plumes for a reason. They are worn by males as badges to impress the females. There are only four of them and they aren't actually tail feathers, but uppertail coverts. They dangle down and are ruffled by the slightest breeze and must make life awkward at times for the male, especially when it is incubating the eggs within the tree hole. Males often leave a perch by dropping backwards.

Nonetheless, the tail varies in length and the best males obviously have the longest ones. The sheer inconvenience is proof of a male's fitness, its ability to cope with life and still grow its ornament. The males show the tail off in a superb display flight in which they rise above the canopy and then fall back down again, calling; the longest-tailed males perform the greatest number of displays. Males also have brilliant scarlet breasts (as if they needed any more bling), and studies have shown that the colour comes from pigments obtained in the diet; the respective brightness may also be reflective of male quality.

All in all, females don't have to be too discerning to assess their potential mates. The work is done for them. They are the real reason that one of the world's most fabulously adorned birds is as stunning as it is.

WEEK 11

Superb starling

Lamprotornis superbus

EAST AFRICA

18cm (7in)

IT'S NOT ONE OF THE GREAT SONGSTERS of the world, but the superb starling makes up for it by being pleasing, lively and indefatigable. In the hot savannahs and thorn scrub of east Africa, where it occurs, it is one of the few birds that sings during the heat of the day, and it's often found around human habitation. Several birds often band together in the shade and give a slower, more halting version of what is on the recording. It is a social break.

In parts of Kenya, superb starlings often feed in the same places, and at the same time, as vervet monkeys (*Chlorocebus pygerythrus*) and they both spend much time on the ground. Studies have shown that the monkeys have learned to respond to the alarm calls of the starlings and are able to distinguish between that given for an aerial predator, such as an eagle, which is higher pitched, and that of a ground predator, such as a leopard. This knowledge, for the primates, can be the difference between reacting in time to the danger, or being killed. Infant monkeys acquire the knowledge and experience over time. Since the vervet monkeys also have their own highly specific alarm calls, it is reasonable to assume that the starlings react in kind to theirs, too, in a harmonious bird-mammal interaction.

Superb starlings are also highly co-operative among their own kind, particularly in their breeding behaviour. They are group breeders, and chicks may be fed by multiple helpers, not only other adults, but also by young birds. Each pair has its own nest, and only one female lays its clutch of four bluish eggs in the nest, but when they hatch, various members of the group join in for the 4–7 weeks the chicks spend there, which must help a great deal. Some nests only have the odd helper, but as many as 12 have been recorded feeding a particularly pampered brood. Remarkably, young birds may start helping at another nest only a month after fledging themselves. This happens because the superb starling has a particularly long breeding season. In one instance, six females nested 22 times between them in the space of nine months. Despite all the help, however, their nesting success is fairly low.

The spirit of co-operation among these group living birds sometimes goes a little overboard, in that neighbours of the opposite sex frequently take advantage of the proximity, and extra-pair copulations are frequent – in one study, about 14 per cent of chicks were not related to the female's 'official' mate. This behaviour is common in many colonial birds.

Superb starlings, socialites to a tee, also form associations with other species of birds, mostly various weavers, especially the white-headed buffalo-weaver (*Dinemellia dinemelli*), and other starling species. Weavers feed primarily on seeds, while the superb starling is largely insectivorous, so presumably they don't compete. In common with other members of the family, superb starlings have an unusual feeding method known as prying, in which they insert their bill in the ground and then open it, providing access to whatever is in the soil. They also feed from the surface, and take all manner of other items, including fruit and nectar. They regularly take scraps at campgrounds and villages.

When they are breeding, the starlings' association with buffalo-weavers may turn unpleasant, with the starlings taking over nests constructed by the latter. The starlings may even remove the eggs of the weavers during the eviction, and the weavers may occasionally reciprocate.

More often than not, however, the starlings build their own nests, an untidy structure of thorny twigs. These are domed, with a side entrance. Interestingly, if the birds are forced to nest in a less well-protected tree, they will gather thorns from a nearby plant and make a barricade around it.

WEEK 12

Screaming piha

Lipaugus vociferans

SOUTH AMERICA

24–26cm (9½–10¼in)

THE ENGLISH NAME FOR THIS BIRD IS APT: it screams, and it goes 'pi-ha!', or at least 'pi-iya'.

You have almost certainly heard the voice. It is the staple soundtrack for documentaries on the Amazon or for any movies involving jungles. And there's nothing fake about that; the screaming piha is a very common Amazonian bird, and you would be hard-pressed not to hear one if you went there. It is one of the dominant sounds of the whole region.

The piha's advertising call is one of the loudest in the world. It has been measured at 116 decibels, second only to another bird in the same Cotingidae family, the white bellbird (*Procnias albus*). The latter's call reaches 125 decibels, and there is much speculation among scientists as to why the bird doesn't deafen itself with its own vocalisation. Meanwhile, to hear a screaming piha up close is the equivalent of a nearby siren or a loud rock band, and it can be genuinely harmful to the human ear. The sound can carry through 300m (1000ft) of dense tropical forest.

Not surprisingly, such a familiar sound has spawned local legends. In Guyana, it is known as the 'gold bird', because it is believed that if you follow it through the forest, you will find a pot of gold. A similar legend in Brazil says that it will lead you to rubber trees, again to guarantee a fortune. So at least you damage your hearing for a reason. A highly accurate rendition is the Brazilian local name *cricrió*.

You might find gold by following a screaming piha, but setting eyes on the bird itself is every bit as difficult. It is an extraordinarily drab bird, with sluggish habits, and it stays in the mid-storey of dense forests, rarely at the edges or in open areas, and not showing itself easily. An illustration of its secretive lifestyle is that only a handful of nests have ever been found. These comprise platforms of thin sticks strewn between two parallel branches. Just a single creamy egg comprises the clutch.

The piha's advertising call is one of the loudest in the world. It has been measured at 116 decibels, second only to another bird in the same Cotingidae family, the white bellbird (Procnias albus).

Within the forest, male screaming pihas arrange themselves in clusters. Each has a territory of its own, and each spends much of the day (77 per cent in one study) sitting on a perch about 5–8m (16–26ft) above ground, dedicating its efforts, as described so delightfully by John Kricher in *The New Neotropical Companion* (2008), to 'exploding with its voice.' The effort is formidable. The bird makes a set of gentle winding-up calls then tips its head back sharply, its mouth fully open to thrust out the loud part of the call.

In a typical setting, about ten male pihas all call from the same area, out of view of one another, but all within hearing range. They are calling in competition. The display is equivalent to a lek, as seen in manakins (see page 44) and the Andean cock-of-the-rock (see page 164) – a group of males competing for the attention of the local females. However, they are more spread out than most lekking birds, and the arrangement is known as an 'exploded lek'. Intriguingly, males seem to be able to space out the calls, so that not all the birds speak at once; they are clearly listening and coordinating. Each male tends to give about 2–3 exclamations per minute, but this sometimes rises to more than ten.

It is for the females to sort out the males they prefer. How they do this is unknown, since there doesn't seem to be much room for an exciting repertoire within an essentially three-note blast. Perhaps they are impressed by effort, or perhaps, quite literally, by volume. The drab plumage does suggest that the sound is the deal-breaker.

But like the legend, if they acquire a good mate, the females will unearth a pot of gold.

WEEK 13

Black-faced solitaire

Myadestes melanops

CENTRAL AMERICA

16–19cm (6¼–7½in)

 NOT MANY BIRD SONGS WILL STOP YOU IN your tracks. But if you are fortunate enough to be trekking through the cloud forests of Central America, there are several species that do just that. These are the solitaires, thrush-like birds with songs that are so pure and perfect that they seem to radiate down from a higher power. Whatever you are doing, you simply have to stop and listen. The forest becomes their theatre and, as they sing, the metaphorical lights go down and the audience is reduced to an awestruck hush.

   Anyone familiar with the finest North American songsters, such as the wood thrush (*Hylocichla mustelina*) or hermit thrush (*Catharus guttatus*), will detect a similarity to solitaire songs. But if anything, the solitaires show a clearer diction, each phrase utterly perfect, rather than revelling in a wide repertoire, as those thrushes do. The black-faced solitaire's song could be boiled down to this single phrase: 'There you, there you go ... dear, sweet one.'

Indeed, as put so aptly by the celebrated ornithologist Dr Paul Slud in his 1964 book *The Birds of Costa Rica: Distribution and Ecology*, it is quality over quantity.

'Stressing virgin clarity of tone instead of vocal pyrotechnics, this solitaire is surely one of the most refined singers of this or any country.'

He is right about another thing, too:

'The disembodied song, hanging in the air like an echo, its struck-crystal timbre harmonizing with the chill surroundings, is almost impossible to trace.'

Attempting to see any solitaire is an absolute nightmare. When singing, the bird tends to stay hidden in the canopy. It isn't brightly coloured and, in contrast to most birds of the cloud forests, it is lethargic and doesn't move around much. The fruitless search, of course, adds to the magic, the voice disembodied, mysterious and ethereal.

The black-faced solitaire has a restricted range in just two countries, Costa Rica and Panama. Although both countries possess large amounts of protected areas, away from these the solitaire is threatened by the cage bird trade and by deforestation. It breeds from April to June across a fairly narrow altitudinal range between 750m (2500ft) and 3000m (10,000ft). But after breeding it breaks the altitudinal shackles and can be seen as low as 100m (330ft) above sea level, an extreme form of altitudinal migration that is typical of these mountainous countries. Outside the breeding season it also becomes sociable, far from its lone-voice 'solitaire' reputation, and may be seen in flocks at suitable food sources.

Curiously for a member of the thrush family, a group renowned for their omnivorous nature, the black-faced solitaire would appear to rely almost entirely on fruit. A bird in captivity was offered copious insects but refused them all, although there is evidence that the birds do reluctantly eat the odd arthropod. It just goes to show how rich tropical forests are, providing fruit all year round, something that isn't possible in temperate regions.

This species feeds mainly in the mid-canopy, plucking fruits and berries while perched. It also makes sallying movements, flying up to pick out-of-reach fruits at the end of branches, often hovering elegantly as it does so.

It also makes sallying movements, flying up to pick out-of-reach fruits at the end of branches, often hovering elegantly as it does so.

Very little is known about its breeding behaviour, other than the fact that it is territorial, and both sexes sing. It builds a cup-shaped nest, mostly out of moss, which it places in a crevice 1–5m (3¼–16½ft) above the ground, often in a bank. Not many nests have been found and, if it wasn't for the exquisite song, this would be just another obscure tropical forest bird.

WEEK 14

Brown wood-owl

Strix leptogrammica

INDIA, SOUTHEAST ASIA AND NEARBY ISLANDS

39–55cm (15½–21½in)

AFTER HEARING AND READING ABOUT MANY a weird sound in this book, here is something much more familiar. It is perhaps a little reassuring to know that there are some vocalizations that are the same wherever you go in the world, and the gorgeous deep hooting of owls is one of these. The brown wood-owl is a widespread species that occurs over much of southern Asia. The recording for this entry is its delicious treble hoot, which may remind American readers of the great horned owl (*Bubo virginianus*).

The brown wood-owl is a deep forest species, including primary rainforest. It has a refreshing aversion to humanity and is therefore rarely seen. Although owls are celebrated for being night birds, many species concentrate their activity at dawn and dusk. Not so this wood owl. This is a proper nocturnal animal. In common with most species inclined this way, it has black eyes, although nobody has worked out why. The least nocturnal owls tend to have yellow eyes.

This owl has a broad diet, although it specializes on mammals. One study of prey brought to the nest showed about 85 per cent mammals, principally rodents, especially rats and squirrels. It also eats birds, lizards and insects, and there are some reports of it catching fish. Its main method of feeding is dropping down from a perch onto something it has heard or seen. It often hunts in the vicinity of glades or tracks, where prey might wander into open areas, making it easier to catch.

Owls are extremely territorial birds, which is part of the reason why they make such loud, far-carrying sounds. Species such as the brown wood-owl may live for many years in the same place, and over time they become familiar with all the best hunting perches and richest density of prey. It isn't an easy living, and without this knowledge, an owl displaced by a rival, for example, often doesn't survive for very long.

They have much more complex outer ears than other birds, although we cannot see them because they are covered with feathers.

Owls are famous for their night-time adaptations to hunting, and while their eyes are the most obvious attribute, these hunters are limited by the amount of light that is actually available. Low light, especially within forests, allows very limited spatial resolution. Humans have surprisingly good night vision, and that of a strictly nocturnal owl in exactly the same conditions is only about 2.7 times as bright as ours. However, their eyes are over 100 times more sensitive in low light than those, for example, of a pigeon.

One of the greatest advantages owls have in low light is their hearing, and in this they have exceptional gifts, way ahead of most of their class. They have much more complex outer ears than other birds, although we cannot see them because they are covered with feathers. What they do is increase the distance between the ears on the head; directional detection, in ourselves and owls, is achieved by the perception of the minute difference between the arrival of a sound to one ear as compared to the other. If a sound comes from the right, it is detected by the right ear fractionally quicker than the left, and the differential gives us the information as to its direction. By having ear openings well apart, owls are more sensitive to this than other birds.

Remarkably, most owls also have asymmetric ear openings, meaning that one ear is slightly higher on the skull than the other. This means that soundwaves coming from above or below will enter one ear fractionally sooner than the other, and this confers vertical information to add to the owl's horizontal information already described. It has, in other words, three-dimensional hearing.

The brown wood-owl and other owls mainly find their prey, therefore, by the sound of rustling on the forest floor or nearby branches. Their directional hearing is so good that they can pinpoint their next meal by sound alone, accurate to within a few degrees. Together with stars in the sky and a very good knowledge of their territory, they are fantastically effective hunters.

WEEK 15

Fire-tailed sunbird

Aethopyga ignicauda

NORTH-EAST INDIA EAST TO CHINA AND MYANMAR
MALE 15–20cm (6–8in), FEMALE 8.5–11cm (3½–4½in)

IT'S ACTIVE, IT'S BRILLIANTLY COLOURED and it feeds on nectar. Most people might credit that description to a hummingbird, but the world is full of nectar feeders that aren't hummingbirds. Those famous miniatures are restricted as breeding birds to the Americas, but there are two other major families that also specialize in nectarivory. In Australasia there are the honeyeaters (Meliphagidae), and throughout Africa and Asia there are the sunbirds (Nectariniidae). The latter are often as jewel-like as their more famous counterparts.

There is one intriguing difference, though. Neither honeyeaters nor sunbirds habitually hover to feed, although some sunbirds do occasionally. So, while the Americas are full of blooms that are coevolved to be pollinated by hummingbirds, Old World blooms have to provide perches and be somewhat more robust. However, if you wish to see sunbirds, you must find flowers. And to find a fire-tailed sunbird, one of the most beautiful members of the family, you need to find high-altitude rhododendron forest and meadows, above 3000m (10,000ft) in the Himalayas and nearby ranges. It is quite a setting for quite a bird. Not surprisingly, many of the flowers in these Himalayan slopes depend on sunbirds for their pollination.

Sunbirds gather nectar in a slightly different way to hummingbirds, by sucking at nectar, rather than licking it in rapidly with the tongue. A sunbird's tongue is forked and the edges are intricately frayed at their ends, so the nectar is forced in by capillary action. The nectar is then pumped down the tubular part of the tongue and into two grooves in the palate and then into the intestine. Sunbirds have no crop and, unlike hummers, are unable to store nectar. They must, in effect, barely stop feeding all day.

In common with hummingbirds, the diet is supplemented by insects. Most sunbirds take a lot, and the fire-tailed is no exception. It often makes rapid sallies into the crisp mountain air to snatch at a passing flying insect, and it also comes across various invertebrates, including spiders, in the course of its usual bloom-searching.

The fire-tailed sunbird builds a domed structure out of moss and bark, which is held together with cobwebs.

A diet of nectar and breeding as high as 4800m (15,750ft) ensures that the fire-tailed sunbird must evacuate the highest parts of its range in winter, so it moves downhill in winter and also makes some linear movements, for instance into northern Myanmar. One fortunate observer counted 3300 of these stunning birds on a single morning on a ridge in Yunnan, China, one November day. The rest of us would be happy enough just to catch a glimpse of one!

Although sunbirds are less famous and celebrated than hummingbirds, they easily outdo them by building much more elaborate nests, as opposed to the modest cups of their rivals. The fire-tailed sunbird builds a domed structure out of moss and bark, which is held together with cobwebs. There is a side entrance, and the interior is stuffed with plant down, grass and feathers. It is decorated on the outside with a variety of material, including moss, in order to break up the shape. The whole construction, entirely the work of the female, is suspended from a branch or even a leaf, which makes it harder to reach for predators.

Another difference between sunbirds and hummingbirds is that, while much hummingbird colouration is structural, with the feathers being essentially colourless, the colouration of sunbirds generally comes from pigments, allowing a profusion of yellows and reds. The fire-tailed sunbird is a veritable kaleidoscope of pigments, making it one of the gaudiest in the whole family.

WEEK 16

Northern carmine bee-eater

Merops nubicus

SAHEL BELT OF AFRICA

24–27cm (9½–10½in)

SHOULD YOU EVER HEAR THE 'RUK, RUK' call featured on the recording here, look up. The chances are that above your head will appear one of the most elegant, charismatic and improbably coloured African birds. It's a bird that looks like it should come down from the clouds, and that's exactly what it does.

The northern carmine bee-eater lives a highly aerial lifestyle, catching fast insects in the skies above treetop height. With its long, pointed wings, long tail and slim body, it is adapted to spend much of its time aloft, frequently at an altitude between 50–100m (160–330ft), and its facility in the air is a pure joy to observe. Using fast wingbeats to accelerate, it rises effortlessly, turns on a sixpence, glides, jinks and does everything it needs to catch prey turbocharged by the heat. Remarkably, it manages to grab insects with the very tip of its long, curved bill, and the bill has rigid edges so that all the force is concentrated there. It easily crushes the exoskeletons of most of its prey. Larger insects, up to 4cm (1½in) long, are brought down to a perch, where the bee-eater beats them to a pulp before swallowing their shattered bodies. This species eats a variety of grasshoppers, locusts, bees, wasps, dragonflies, dung beetles and ants.

Carmine bee-eaters have several unexpected party tricks. One is to use large animals, and humans on occasion, as 'beaters', to flush flying insects from the long grass and into the bee-eater's range. Among the many animals it is known to use are zebra, cattle, gazelles and camels. It also follows large birds such as storks, ostrich (*Struthio camelus*), cranes, secretary bird (*Sagittarius serpentarius*) and, quite frequently, bustards such as the kori bustard (*Ardeotis kori*). It will often perch on the back of these animals, dashing off to catch a meal and then hitching a ride. They have also been known to follow cars and trucks in flight, swooping on whatever is disturbed by the traffic. It is a remarkable piece of opportunism.

Another trick, used by quite a range of tropical insectivorous birds, is to be attracted to bushfires. Quite fearlessly, they circle the area and fly into the smoke, daringly close to the flames, taking advantage of the fleeing insects, not entirely different to the feeding method of the ocellated antbird (see page 16).

Even more surprisingly, carmine bee-eaters will dive down into the water with a splash, often to take a bath, but at least occasionally they have been known to catch small fish in this way. They have even been seen to immerse themselves completely.

Northern and southern (*M. nubicoides*) carmine bee-eaters are among the most popular of all African birds, which is hardly surprising given their lavish plumage colouration and elegance. What makes them more popular still is their habit of nesting in dense breeding colonies along rivers, using vertical banks. There are dozens of hotspots where you can see these birds, year after year, as they tend to return to the same place for each breeding attempt. Northern carmine bee-eaters are just beginning to breed at the moment, in April. The birds dig out their own chambers; for this reason, they have strong feet and claws.

Carmine bee-eaters will dive down into the water with a splash, often to take a bath, but at least occasionally they have been known to catch small fish in this way.

Carmine bee-eater colonies are often remarkably dense, with up to 60 burrows per square metre (10 sq. ft) recorded in vertical cliffs. And some colonies may hold hundreds, or even thousands of pairs. For a bird that is used to flying up in the air, with unlimited space, this must be quite a change.

For a human visitor, seeing thousands of these elegant forms, coming and going, gliding and twisting, their plumage ablaze, is one of the great experiences of birding in the tropics.

WEEK 17

Purple-crowned fairywren

Malurus coronatus

NORTHERN AUSTRALIA

14–15cm (5½–6in)

IF YOU HEAR ONE PURPLE-CROWNED fairywren, you hear several. The high-pitched reeling song, as heard in this recording, is typically sung as a duet, and the 'chet-chet' calls are always collective. In common with many tropical species, these fairywrens live in groups. The groups are very close, both physically and socially. The members barely leave each other's side throughout their lives, maintaining these constant calls over the hours and days. The group dynamic is exceptionally stable, with many birds remaining in the same group for years. Leaving is as big an event as human children leaving for university.

The fairywrens are among the most popular of Australia's birds. The superb fairywren (*M. cyaneus*) and the splendid fairywren (*M. splendens*) – adjectives were clearly in short supply when they named them – are both quite common garden birds in Australian cities, and those species are clad in brilliant iridescent blue colours. All species are relatively tiny, with rotund bodies and an extremely long tail, which they often hold up at an angle like a Eurasian wren (*Troglodytes troglodytes*). Although they spend much time hidden in dense vegetation close to the ground, they are insatiably curious and sprightly, so many Australians are familiar with them.

The purple-crowned fairywren is an outlier, restricted to the margins of rivers in the tropical north. It lives in tall grass and *Pandanus* (screw pine) bushes, and it has particularly strong feet that enable it to manoeuvre around and hold on to their narrow, sturdy, barbed leaves. It often builds its bulky nest, an oval 10cm (4in) or so in diameter, in the leaf-axils of these plants. It is routine for random leaf litter to accumulate in the same axils, affording potentially excellent camouflage.

If a fairywren nest is threatened, the adults do something quite extraordinary. They become theatrical. They lower their head and neck and press their tail down so that it scrapes the ground; they ruffle their feathers and, in contrast to their usual hop, they will begin running on the ground, always away from the nest. This is an extraordinary distraction display designed to catch the attention of predators ('What on earth is that?') and lure them away from the vulnerable chicks. The display is known as a 'rodent run', because the birds behave like mice.

Extensive studies on fairywrens have revealed that the relationships between members of the group are complex. Most units consist of a breeding pair with one or more young birds, almost always the pair's progeny from one or more previous years. The groups may have up to seven members, but only the senior male and female breed. Indeed, young males may retain juvenile plumage for several years while they accompany their parents. Eventually, as mentioned above, the youngsters leave the group to join up with a nearby one.

While in the group, the youngsters act as helpers. When the senior pair are attempting to nest, these auxiliaries are expected to help feed the young, both in the nest and when the new brood has fledged. They are expected to help with defence of the territory, and they also take part in the rodent run, described above. They remain in servitude until they break out to find their own life.

The bond between the senior male and female is long-lasting for such a small bird; indeed, it is almost always lifelong. The divorce rate is only 1.7 per cent, at least from one study, and more than 50 per cent of pairs were found to be intact from one year to the next. The pair bond is reinforced by constant duetting and mutual defence of the territory.

There is, however, a curious underlying trend. All the fairywrens studied so far have extraordinarily high rates of extrapair paternity – in other words, despite their close proximity and stability, pairs are not sexually 'faithful' to one another. In the superb fairywren, 76 per cent of all young were found to be fathered by a male outside the group – that's the highest rate recorded for any bird.

It appears that, in the pre-dawn darkness, male fairywrens take excursions outside the territory and solicit to neighbouring females. Some individuals even bring colourful flower petals to make a good impression, as well as singing and displaying.

The solidity in a fairywren group, therefore, isn't quite what it seems.

WEEK 18

Red-billed oxpecker

Buphagus erythrorynchus

EASTERN AND SOUTHERN AFRICA

20cm (8in)

 IF YOU'VE EVER BEEN FORTUNATE ENOUGH to go on safari in Africa, you might notice that a certain bird is photobombing many of your images of large mammals. It can almost always be seen on the backs of large, grazing herbivores such as giraffes and larger antelopes. It also, somewhat riskily, feeds from the backs of hippos, which could dive at any moment, using its strong claws to hold on.

This remarkable bird is the red-billed oxpecker; there is a second species, the yellow-billed oxpecker (*B. africanus*) with a very similar ecology. Oxpeckers don't have a habitat as such; they spend all day riding bareback. Only at dusk do they retreat, often in large numbers, to roost in reedbeds or trees. And of course, you cannot nest on a moving animal, although if oxpeckers could, they would certainly try.

The attraction of animal hides is, of course, food. There are two enormous advantages to finding sustenance there. Firstly, there aren't many competitors, although a number of species are part time hide-riders. Secondly, there is an awful lot of food on the fur of large mammals and, in places, plenty of options. It is a remarkably stable environment, and not a day goes by without an oxpecker doing its thing, unless it is looking after young in the nest.

It can almost always be seen on the backs of large, grazing herbivores such as giraffes and larger antelopes.

What, though, do oxpeckers find so nourishing about fur? You might be surprised to learn that it is ticks. There is a variety of other fauna that fills up the menu at times, including blackflies, horseflies (and their maggots), lice and leeches (are you itching yet?). But none of these are as important as ticks. Oxpeckers even prefer certain species and sizes of ticks, those from the speciality menu.

If you've ever had ticks, you will know how difficult they are to remove, burying their mouthparts in the skin. The oxpecker can use its bill simply to pluck them out, but on longer hair it uses a scissor-type motion, manoeuvring its head to the side to get a good grip. It is clearly this expert service that, over the years, makes animals tolerate oxpeckers. Presumably, most animals could harass the birds if they wanted to, and a number of mammals, notably elephants, cannot stand them. The latter are said to have sensitive skin, although this may not be the reason.

Interestingly, ticks themselves aren't particularly good meals, no better than any other invertebrate. But what makes them irresistible to oxpeckers is that when they are engorged with blood, they provide a hyper-nutritious meal. You could, therefore, say that oxpeckers are vampire-like bloodsuckers, and they don't dispel this reputation by regularly feeding at open wounds and lapping up the blood. Having said that, they don't pick at wounds to make them bleed more, and their liking for body fluids also stretches to mucus from the eyes and mouth, and also ear wax. No self-respecting vampire would be seen dead feeding on those.

Since oxpeckers spend all day on animal fur, much of their social life also takes place there, too. Courting oxpeckers meet across a crowded hide, and it would take far too much effort to slope away somewhere else to consummate their relationship, so they copulate onboard, too. It is a wild ride – blood, sex and tears. The birds actually nest in tree holes, and guess what they use to line their nests? Fur, of course, which they pluck from their hosts.

The life of oxpeckers is so obviously successful that you wonder why there are only two species. Perhaps long ago, where there were many more places with decent populations of megafauna, they or something else occupied this niche more widely.

As for the hosts themselves, you can guess that they become seriously familiar with the oxpeckers' harsh call notes. Indeed, some animals look up when the birds make alarm calls. But they must be part of their own life's soundtrack.

WEEK 19

Oilbird

Steatornis caripensis
NORTHERN AND WESTERN SOUTH AMERICA
45–49cm (17–19½in)

 **OKAY, YOU PROBABLY DIDN'T BUY A BOOK** on tropical birdsong in order to listen to a sound that could be likened to a gathering of drunks violently spitting out a beer they don't like. The gasping and frothing aren't at all pleasant to listen to. The Spanish name for this bird is onomatopoeic: *guácharo*.

But the oilbird has a remarkable acoustic talent, which you can also hear on the recording. The odd click you pick up is highly significant. This is one of the world's most remarkable bird sounds. The clicks are the bird's sonar and are used for echolocation. The oilbird lives and breeds in caves, where there is never any natural light at all. It breeds on ledges within the cave and needs to be able to move around freely. So it uses clicks in the range 1.5–2.5 hertz, which echo back from the walls and from other birds to ensure that it doesn't bump into things and injure itself. The clicks are in our audible range, and the oilbird doesn't even approach the echolocation performance of bats, which can avoid minute objects in complete darkness. The best an oilbird can do is an object about 20cm (8in) in diameter (a rival study suggested 3cm (1¼in)), but whatever the actual figure, these large birds with rounded wings clearly cope perfectly well. They are highly colonial; one cave contains over 10,000 nests, and many others contain hundreds. They obviously manage to avoid widespread carnage.

Only two sorts of birds in the world use echolocation. The others are swiftlets (Apodidae), which also nest in caves. However, the oilbird is unique in also being nocturnal. It leaves its caves after dark to feed, and it returns at dawn. Some oilbirds simply never see the light of day.

The oilbird, which is similar to a large member of the nightjar family (Caprimulgidae), with its small bill, large head and huge gape, as well as long tail and brown plumage, is also unique in another way. It is the world's only nocturnal fruit-eating bird. It doesn't eat anything else. At night it flies to fruiting trees and plucks fruit while in a mid-air hover. It swallows them whole and they enter the bird's oesophagus, where the fleshy pulp is torn away from the seed or seeds. The seeds are eventually regurgitated, so the oilbird acts as a major disperser of forest trees.

It is the world's only nocturnal fruit-eating bird. It doesn't eat anything else. At night it flies to fruiting trees and plucks fruit while in a mid-air hover.

The oilbird often flies many kilometres over lowland and montane forest to find fruiting trees, sometimes up to 120km (75 miles) a night. But how does it find its food in the dark? You might think it uses echolocation, but in fact it 'switches this off' when it leaves the cave. Firstly, it uses vision. It turns out that the oilbird has astonishingly sensitive eyes; its image brightness at night is four times as strong as a human's and even 1.5 times greater than that even of an owl. It achieves this by having the highest density of light-sensitive rod cells of any vertebrate, nearly a million rods per square millimetre. This approaches the theoretical limits of visual sensitivity, although the image produced is low in spatial resolution.

The other sense that an oilbird uses to hunt is smell. Oilbirds have a strong olfactory capability and there is no doubt that they can detect plumes of odour emanating from ripening fruits – indeed, many fruits would be very difficult to find by sight, even in the relatively open forest canopy. Thus, it is a remarkably sensory bird that uses hearing, vision and smell to drive its entirely unique lifestyle. There is no species in the world quite like it.

WEEK 20

Indian cuckoo

Cuculus micropterus

INDIA AND EAST ASIA

32–35cm (12½–13in)

OF ALL THE SONGS IN THIS BOOK, FEW FIT so easily into the western musical lexicon than that of the Indian cuckoo. The clear, four-note phrase has a slightly mysterious air and could easily be transcribed directly on to the soundtrack of a movie, or even form the basis of a song. Perhaps somebody has already used it? The refrain also gives itself easily to memory phrases, of which the best known is 'crossword puzzle', with another popular one being 'orange pekoe'. Not surprisingly, the call has been rendered in many local languages. In Nepal, where it is a familiar spring song, it is aptly rendered 'kafal peko', meaning 'the kafal fruit is ripe'.

At any rate, when so many bird songs are hard to remember, this one is a joy for the birding beginner.

The Indian cuckoo has a wide range, occurring from the evergreen rainforests of tropical Southeast Asia to the temperate deciduous forests of the Himalaya and southern Russia. In the northern part of its range, it is a migrant and is only heard in the spring, while further south it is heard any time from late December to the following August. The migrant birds and the residents thus have a starkly and strikingly different lifestyle, and you are forced to wonder whether they are significantly genetically different.

One thing that most certainly does vary is the host species, because this, like the very similar common cuckoo (*C. canorus*), is a brood parasite, laying its eggs in the nests of other species and subcontracting the work of bringing up its own young. In different parts of its range, it uses different birds to do its dirty work. In Russia, it is mainly the brown shrike (*Lanius cristatus*), while in India it is mainly a group of birds called drongos, especially the very abundant black drongo (*Dicrurus macrocercus*). In China it has been known to be a parasite of the azure-winged magpie (*Cyanopica cyanus*).

The common cuckoo tends to use hosts that are much smaller than itself and not much of a threat, but when the female Indian cuckoo lays her egg in the nest of a host, she is putting herself at serious risk.

What is striking about these hosts is that none of them is exactly meek and mild. All of them can stand up for themselves, and can be decidedly aggressive, even predatory. The common cuckoo tends to use hosts that are much smaller than itself and not much of a threat, but when the female Indian cuckoo lays her egg in the nest of a host, she is putting herself at serious risk. In order to cater for this, the male and female work as a team: the male making itself obvious and distracting the attention of the hosts, while the female steals in during the commotion. The female then takes a host egg and eats it, keeping the clutch size the same. To complete the deception, the female will lay an egg of similar colour and pattern to the host.

Once laid, though, the egg of the Indian cuckoo is a bomb to its host's breeding attempt. In the nest of shrikes, the Indian cuckoo chick hatches in 12 days (that's because the chick starts growing when still in the female cuckoo's oviduct) and the shrike chicks hatch in 14 days, giving the parasite a significant head start. It isn't yet known whether Indian cuckoo chicks evict the eggs or nestlings of their host, as the common cuckoo chick does, but its extra two days of attention does ensure that the Indian cuckoo chick can potentially outcompete its foster siblings, often causing their demise. The parasite nestlings make very similar calls to those of their host species, ensuring that they have the lion's share of any food offerings.

Away from the nest, the Indian cuckoo follows the style of many other species in its family by having an unusual diet, comprising various foods avoided by other birds. In particular, it has a fondness for hairy caterpillars, many of which have noxious hairs and a taste that is intended to repel predators. It also eats butterflies, many of which also contain chemical deterrents.

To be an Indian cuckoo, you have to be tough.

WEEK 21

Eastern paradise-whydah

Vidua paradisaea

EASTERN AND SOUTHERN AFRICA

13–14cm (5–5½in), MALE IN BREEDING PLUMAGE 36–39cm (14–15½in)

 IT'S A PRETTY SOLID RULE FOR A SINGING bird that you must sing the 'correct' song. It's fine to have a wide repertoire to impress rivals and suitors alike, but if you launch too far out of the norm, your intended audience – those of your own species – might not recognize you as their own. So, it is essential that you always self-identify as the species that you are. Flourishes are fine, inventiveness is fine. Mimicry is also fine, so long as it's in the right context and you only use it to embellish your recognizable song. Don't be too clever.

This is a solid rule for 99 per cent of the world's birds. But this is the natural world, so there is always an exception. A very peculiar group of seed-eating birds known as whydahs and indigobirds are the outliers. Take the eastern paradise-whydah. If a male of this species wants to woo a female, it needs to sing the song of something completely different – the melba finch, the green-winged pytilia (*Pytilia melba*). This small seed-eater isn't even in the same family as the whydah.

Nonetheless, it is incumbent upon the males to be perfect imitators. The melba finches don't make it easy for them, either; they have dialects, which means that a given finch will sing a different song to its neighbours from another district. The whydah must imitate the correct song, or the females won't be interested.

The reason for this odd state of affairs is that eastern paradise-whydahs are brood parasites, and their hosts are melba finches. They do not reproduce in any other way, and never raise their own young. Each female lays eggs inside the finch's nest, and several females may lay in the same nest. Nonetheless, the finch usually raises both species together, albeit normally with fewer of its own kind than in an unaffected nest. It's just as well that the host young can coexist with the whydahs, because in some cases as many as 50 per cent of nests are parasitized.

So the whydah follows the melba finch's life, and becomes the ornithological version of a catfish. It times its breeding season to coincide, and it is stimulated to lay eggs when it hears the finch's song. Females sometimes lay eggs when the finches are singing but the males aren't. They also spend large amounts of time watching the melba finches building their nest, to make sure that they are ready. Even the nestling paradise-whydahs imitate the begging calls of the host species. It is all very weird and shadowy.

The display of the male eastern paradise-whydah is also intriguing, not least because it is only performed a couple of times a day, once at about 10am and again at 4pm. Each 'performance' lasts for about 20 minutes, and that's it. It's worth seeing though, and presumably the females don't need to see any more. The male paradise-whydah has an extremely long tail, in which two feathers are twisted at 90 degrees to make a 'bulge', somewhat resembling ornate, old-fashioned dresses. This bling is best shown off during a flight display.

Performed in terrain with scattered bushes, the display consists of males flying up at a sharp angle to reach a height of 20–30m (65–100ft). Once in the air, they circle and hold up their central tail feathers. They give off a few call notes and then descend to a perch, whereupon they sing the melba finch's song.

Why the females don't just assess the males on the strength of their display and their own song, no one knows. It is a life borne of plagiarism.

The whydah follows the melba finch's life, and becomes the ornithological version of a catfish.

WEEK 22

Blue whistling-thrush

Myophonus caeruleus

SOUTHEAST ASIA AND MOUNTAINS OF INDIA,
PAKISTAN AND AFGHANISTAN

29–35cm (11½–13¾in)

WHEN YOU TUNE INTO THE RECORDING OF this bird, close your eyes and imagine the scene. The clear, fluty, slightly slurred, lark-like whistles are emanating from a rocky gully above a tumbling mountain stream. Vast, snowy peaks dominate the horizon, and the air has an invigorating zing. Just above, dense conifer woods hold shiny Himalayan avian treasures. But for now, your attention is upon the singer itself, a dark thrush with a brilliant yellow bill, and all over-royal blue plumage with iridescent bead-like spangles.

'Hold on,' you might say. 'This is a book about tropical birds, not about mountain birds.' And you'd be right – and that's the paradox. The lovely blue whistling-thrush is one of many tropical birds that leads something of a double life. Yes, it is at home here in the Himalayan hinterland, breeding anywhere between 1000m and 4000m

(3300–13,000ft), and in the highest regions will migrate downhill in the winter. However, this very same species is equally at home in the mangroves of Malaysia at sea level, or on garden lawns in Hong Kong, China. In many parts of the range, it is a forest bird, although it is seldom far from rocky places and rivers. In short, it isn't easy to pin down. Most people think of tropical birds as being soft and unadaptable. The blue whistling-thrush, and many others, prove that this isn't so.

Of course, to be adaptable you need what you might call a transferable ecology, and the thrush family (Turdidae) has spread successfully all over the world, combining foraging for ground invertebrates with taking berries off trees and shrubs. In the more specific case of the blue whistling-thrush, most studies suggest that its superpower is in catching and breaking open hard-shelled invertebrates such as crabs and, in particular, snails. It is one of the few birds, along with the European song thrush (*Turdus philomelos*), that uses an anvil, breaking shells against favoured rocks or other hard surfaces, where the discarded fragments of previous destruction build up in piles. In one study, an individual appeared to subsist almost entirely on snails. Presumably, individuals living on the coast subject crabs to the same kind of brutal treatment.

Most people think of tropical birds as being soft and unadaptable. The blue whistling-thrush, and many others, prove that this isn't so.

It isn't confined to this diet, however. It often feeds at the water's edge to catch water beetles and a variety of larvae. The same species is comfortably at home feeding in damp woods, in the midst of shade, turning over leaf litter in a style out of the official thrush handbook.

It often feeds at dusk and dawn, when it is dark. Interestingly, those speckles that are sprinkled over the plumage show ultraviolet reflectance. Most birds have a significant UV sensitivity in their eyes, so the spots will look bright and gleaming to them. It is thought that they are useful in drawing attention to a thrush and showing that a territory is occupied, a signal to rivals.

The blue whistling-thrush usually selects a ledge for its large, bulky, cup nest. This may be on a river bank or small cliff overlooking running water or, very frequently, in a cave – the species is often found in limestone regions, which are often studded with underground hollows. In more urban areas, drainage ditches make an ideal substitute. In high-altitude regions, it often nests on relatively undisturbed buildings, such as temples.

The clutch consists of 2–5 eggs, and in some years a pair may be able to raise two broods. Interestingly, the clutch in tropical regions is usually smaller (2–3), as indeed clutches in tropical areas usually are. This is a good example of this species' remarkable tropical-temperate flexibility.

WEEK 23

Hooded pitohui

Pitohui dichrous

NEW GUINEA

22–23cm (8½–9in)

 **WHEN THE OBSCURE AND ARCANE IS** revealed to be extraordinary, it is a sweet moment. Ornithologically, those of us who adore unusual birds feel a curious validation when the light of discovery makes the object of our passion unexpectedly celebrated. The remarkable biology of the hooded pitohui is a case in point.

Before the 1990s, this bird nestled in the densest undergrowth of obscurity. New Guinea, where the pitohui occurs, is a world apart for most of us, a difficult, expensive and sometimes dangerous place to visit. And most of its birds – and there are many astonishing ones – are overshadowed by the world-famous birds-of-paradise (see pages 40 and 176). The hooded pitohui is certainly attractive, but let's be honest, under ordinary circumstances the great broadcaster

Sir David Attenborough would never have been tempted to New Guinea to make a programme about this sort of bird.

The pitohui began to stray from the ranks of the unexceptional in 1990, when researchers from the California Academy of Sciences, led by ornithologist Jack Dumbacher, were mist netting birds in the island's forests. In their 40 nets, they caught several pitohuis. One, not unreasonably, bit and scratched Dumbacher as he untangled it, and he instinctively put his fingers to his mouth to soothe the pain. Quite unexpectedly, he began to feel numbness and burning around his lips, tongue and finger. Others who had handled the birds and also licked their fingers felt the same. By chance, they had discovered that the hooded pitohui is poisonous.

Of course, the locals knew this already. Their opinion was that the pitohui was bad all round, and not worth eating. After the discovery, several curious museum staff licked the feathers of Pitohui specimens (yes, really, all in the name of science) and found that they felt the same burning sensations.

Later research discovered that the bird's feathers and skin contained a compound that was the same as the homobatrachotoxin found in the poison arrow frogs of South America. These toxins are very dangerous: indigenous peoples rub their arrows on the skin of poison arrow frogs, and once fired into the body of mammals, the effect is both instantaneous and lethal. In the New Guinea pitohuis, however, the toxins are found in such small quantities that they can't do too much damage to humans, at any rate. The bird doesn't produce the poison, either, but instead ingests it from some of the local beetles belonging to the genus *Choresine* (Melyridae).

So, what are the toxins for? It seems highly unlikely that a bird would evolve noxious plumage incidentally. It is thought that they might help the pitohuis to discourage ectoparasites such as lice and ticks from infesting their plumage, as they do many birds. Another possibility is that the poor-tasting plumage affords protection against predators, which learn their colour pattern and avoid them.

Since this unexpected discovery, several other birds have been successfully tested for similar poisons, including other species of pitohui, as well as a number of different birds in New Guinea. The spur-winged goose (*Plectropterus gambensis*) is another, quite unexpected addition, and there are bound to be more. A whole new field of research has opened up.

The bird's feathers and skin contained a compound that was the same as the homobatrachotoxin found in the poison arrow frogs of South America.

Despite its fame, little is still known about the hooded pitohui. The name, not surprisingly, comes from its liquid call-notes, and it feeds on figs, berries and other insects besides beetles. It often joins mixed feeding parties as they move through the forest. It makes a cup-shaped nest out of vines, and it seems that a breeding pair often enlists helpers in the nesting attempt, as do quite a number of tropical birds.

The case of the poisonous pitohui is a delightful reminder that the world is a marvellous place, with exciting discoveries to be made everywhere, even in its most remote corners. The irony, though, is that Jack Dumbacher didn't go to New Guinea to study pitohuis; it was birds-of-paradise, obviously.

WEEK 24

Asian koel

Eudynamys scolopaceus

INDIA, SOUTH-EAST ASIA AND ISLANDS

39–46cm (15½–18in)

IS THERE ANYWHERE IN THE WORLD A noisier bird than the Asian koel? I am asking this following a sleep-deprived trip to Sri Lanka, where every morning the koels replaced any need for a phone alarm. If the males weren't giving their incessant 'ko-el' calls, they were making very loud bubbling noises in cahoots with the females. The koel party never stopped.

The advertising call of this member of the cuckoo family echoes around many parts of Asia, at almost any time of year. It is often uttered in sequence, and there is regularly an acceleration, with each call rising slightly in pitch and expressing an increasing sense of panic.

It is such an atmospheric sound, and so universal, emanating from everywhere from forest edge to urban gardens, that it has entered the fabric of many cultures. In India the koel, most strident in the early part of the year, represents the glorious fullness of spring and hearing it is drenched with romance. It is part of the soundtrack of many Bollywood movies and is sprinkled throughout poetry and literature, so that everyone on the subcontinent associates the koel with joyful human courtship. It is even a common name for women. Few other birds have such cultural cachet.

The human association is long and, potentially, highly intriguing. The koel is mentioned in the Vedas, a famous and very ancient Sanskrit document dated from 2000 BCE. Its name has been transcribed as *anya-vapa* and, if the literal translation is correct, that means 'sown for others to reap'. That could be a reference to the koel's parasitic lifestyle in which, cuckoo-like, the youngsters are raised by foster parents. If so, it pre-dates Aristotle who, in the 3rd century BCE, mentioned that the common cuckoo (*Cuculus canorus*) chick was raised by other birds, usurping it as the first known reference to this lifestyle.

Asian koels differ in many ways in their brood parasitic strategy compared to the well-known common cuckoo. For a start, they have hosts of a very different profile to the small insectivorous species favoured by the Eurasian bird. The most common host in many places is the house crow (*Corvus splendens*, see page 128); in one study in India, 5 per cent of all house crow nests were parasitized. Koels use other crow species, too, and also mynas (Sturnidae), laughingthrushes (*Garrulax* spp.) and shrikes (*Lanius* spp.). Across the range, many species have been recorded. Presumably, as in the case of cuckoos that are well studied, female

Another interesting quirk is that it is common for several female koels to parasitize the same nest, something that is rare in the common cuckoo.

koels raised in a nest of, say, house crows will go on in their breeding life to parasitize that same species.

The biggest difference in strategy, or at least outcome, is that young koels are often raised alongside the chicks of their host. True, the female will often eat a host egg when it raids a nest and true, the young parasites usually hatch before their foster parents' eggs (on average, two days before). However, although the nestlings may attempt to evict the foster siblings, they only rarely succeed, and they don't always outcompete them, either. Thus, it is quite common for koel chicks and crow chicks to be raised from the same nest, presumably despite considerable tension!

Another interesting quirk is that it is common for several female koels to parasitize the same nest, something that is rare in the common cuckoo. It is possible that this happens because koels often breed in dense clusters, and there is simply a shortage of nests. Usually it is only two or three females host-sharing, but an extraordinary case has been recorded in India where a crow nest contained 13 koel eggs, surely a case of overkill where nobody wins.

Whatever the outcome, one thing is for sure. Whether it is koels or house crows that flourish most in a breeding attempt, the resulting progeny will be noisy!

WEEK 25

Malayan banded pitta

Hydrornis irena

PENINSULAR MALAYSIA AND SUMATRA

20–25cm (8–9in)

IT IS QUITE POSSIBLE THAT THE PITTAS (Pittidae) are the most beautiful birds that nobody has ever heard of. Ask anyone in the street to name some tropical stunners, and they will mention hummingbirds, toucans and parrots. But few, if any, will mention pittas.

Yet these birds exhibit a galaxy of gaudy colours and flamboyant patterns that make the jaw drop, even just by looking at paintings or photos. There are red ones, blue ones, green ones, those with spots and bars, and those with patches of orange or yellow. Their plumage is so lavish that you wonder if they aren't the product of artificial intelligence gone mad. If you admire the illustration opposite, you will see what I mean. What are these birds, and where are they?

The answer is that they are shy dwellers on the forest floor of tropical Asia, Africa and northern Australia. What makes them exceptionally unusual among other gemlike wonders is that their bling spends much of its time hidden deep in the shade. These birds don't flaunt their patterns. They are sometimes nicknamed 'jewel-thrushes', but these jewels hide away.

There are about 50 species distributed in tropical forests throughout these regions, although most are found on islands around the Sundas and Indonesia. The Malayan banded pitta is found on Sumatra, as well as neighbouring peninsular Malaysia. It is arguably one of the most beautiful of all pittas.

That's if you can set eyes on it. Among birdwatchers, pittas are famous for being notoriously hard to see. For a thrush-sized bird it is easy to run away on the forest floor, but even if a pitta is in plain sight, it can stay motionless and be overlooked that way. Often the best solution is to creep very quietly towards one that is giving its advertising call. Pittas will often approach if their calls are imitated. The yelping bark of the Malayan banded pitta is quite typical of their vocalizations – loud, to the point and not very variable.

One of the corollaries of being difficult to see is that you are also difficult to study, so pittas have never hit the headlines in regard to some strange piece of weird and wonderful behaviour. In fact, they often act like very average ground-living birds, using their feet and bills to flick away leaf litter while feeding, and taking a predictable range of invertebrates. They hop over the forest floor in long bounds. They have a serious fondness for worms and often carry them in bunches to their chicks in the nests, looking like rotund bodied European blackbirds (*Turdus merula*) or American robins (*T. migratorius*). The Malayan banded pitta does, though, eat a lot of snails. It often picks them up in its bill and breaks the shells against a hard surface, often a tree root or a rock.

The breeding behaviour of pittas also hasn't yet unearthed anything unusual. It seems they are largely monogamous. Usually, a strong sign that a bird is monogamous is when males and females look largely alike (monomorphism); in the most promiscuous species there is rabid sexual selection, with males often much larger and dressed up in fancy plumage. In fact, this pitta shows more dimorphism than most, with the male sporting a gorgeous purple breast and the female showing a pale, closely barred breast. They no doubt know something we don't.

One day, somebody will go mad and study every aspect of pittas' lives. Until then, they remain one of the great unknowns among technicolour tropical birds.

WEEK 26

Bluish-fronted jacamar

Galbula cyanescens

WESTERN AMAZON, SOUTH AMERICA

20–23cm (8–9in)

 HAVE YOU EVER WANDERED THROUGH a tropical forest glade and noticed a bloom of butterflies and wondered to yourself 'I wonder what eats these?'

The answer, in South and Central America at least, is jacamars. These sharp-billed and sharp-eyed birds, small and dashing, are experts in catching insects in mid-air, and their diet encompasses copious butterfly flesh. They have favourite hunting perches, and after a while, a kaleidoscope of colourful wings will appear below these, as well as those of other prey such as dragonflies, bees, wasps and typical flies. Jacamars are found mainly on the edges of forests, by clearings where there is sufficient airspace, and they often hunt next to lakes and rivers.

They are, nonetheless, quite hard to spot. That's because they spend a great deal of time watching and waiting for opportunities before striking. The typical view of a jacamar is of a slim, long-tailed bird perched still, its bill held up at an angle of 70 degrees or so, which presumably gives it the field of view it requires. Prey is invariably caught in mid-air which means that, somewhat curiously, any butterfly that wishes to evade capture has only to land and keep still and it will be safe.

Jacamars resemble bee-eaters (see page 72) in their general shape, although the two groups are unrelated, and bee-eaters spend much more time aloft. However, both groups have long, slender bills with sharp tips. Most birds that catch flying insects, such as swallows and flycatchers of all sorts, have very short bills and a wide gape. Jacamars and bee-eaters, however, do not, and there is some speculation as to why they are different. One possibility is that, because both groups take quite large prey with rapid wingbeats, a long bill keeps struggling invertebrates from damaging the hunter's eyes and face when captured. It's also true that the longer the bill, the faster the tips shut together.

Jacamars resemble bee-eaters in their general shape, although the two groups are unrelated.

In recent years, researchers have found that jacamars can be extremely selective in the prey that they catch. This is necessary because many insects of different types are distasteful, or even poisonous. This includes butterflies. It seems that young jacamars learn this the hard way, by snapping noxious insects and getting their taste buds burned. Over time, they begin to distinguish palatable butterflies from unpalatable species, by sight, often with great precision. Not only do they recognize them in flight before catching them, but they also quickly let go of an insect that they have caught in error. In South America, there are a lot of butterflies fluttering about with tears in their wings.

What is particularly impressive about this is that many palatable butterfly species have evolved to resemble unpalatable ones (known as Müllerian mimicry), and there is good evidence that jacamars are sufficiently sharp-eyed to see through the deception. Furthermore, both the palatable species and their mimics show great regional variation, further confusing the picture. It is thought that, as the prime avian predators of butterflies in neotropical forests, jacamars drive the selection pressure that energizes the mimicry.

In order to catch insects effectively, jacamars need to be territorial so that they aren't disturbed by competitors while hunting. As such, they are noisy, and their ringing calls are a familiar part of the forest-edge soundscape.

WEEK 27

Indian peafowl

Pavo cristatus

INDIA AND SRI LANKA

MALE 1.8–2.3m (6–7½ft), FEMALE 0.9–1m (3–3¼ft)

IF PEAFOWL WERE EVER TO BE ASCRIBED human personality traits, self-doubt would not be one of them. Wherever they occur, either wild in the lowlands of India and Sri Lanka, or in parks in many other parts of the world, these birds strut around with a notable fearlessness. Their call is equally famous, a confident, clanging trumpeting that has two settings, loud and very loud. It carries far and is often part of the atmosphere of temples and national parks of the Subcontinent.

It helps that the peacock, with its lavish, opulent feather train, is sacred in many countries and enmeshed in many cultures. In Hinduism it is often depicted as a mount of the gods, such as the goddess of fertility, Lakshmi and the god of war, Kartikeya, who both ride on a peacock. The famous feathers are often depicted on Lord Krishna's crest. It has royal associations in Buddhism, representing wisdom, and for the Sinhalese it is one of the signs of the zodiac. As such, it is revered in much of its natural range and is generally, although not universally, left alone. It has spread out from its core forest home and become familiar in many rural areas.

What is truly extraordinary in cultural terms is that the peafowl has also become revered far from its natural range. In China, the feathers were greatly admired in the imperial courts, and there are records of robes of peacock feathers worn in the late Qing dynasty in the 17th century. The peacock was introduced to the Middle East in the 10th century BCE, long enough ago to be mentioned in the Bible as a gift to Solomon (1 Kings 10:22), 965–931 BCE. It became an important symbol to the Ancient Greeks, where it represented the goddess Hera. It seems that wherever it went, the peafowl became widely admired to the point of worship.

The famous train, of which the longest feathers are upper tail coverts, not the tail itself, is indeed an example of extravagance, with few equals anywhere in the avian world. The feathers are of several types, the longest of which, those that end with a fishtail shape, can be more than 1m (3¼ft) long. Other feathers end in the famous eyespots, with their glorious iridescence. As everybody knows, in order to show off its train to advantage, the male peafowl, the peacock, spreads all 200 tail coverts out in a fan, one of the great sights of nature. It often shakes the fan, and it also, quite deliberately, angles its train slightly to the sun, so that the female can see the display at peak iridescent glory.

Many studies have puzzled over the wild opulence of the peacock's tail. If you ever watch males displaying to females, the latter almost invariably enter into disinterested mode – 'Do you think I haven't seen all this before?' In one experiment the eyes were blackened and the poor male's breeding success nosedived, so at least all this bling counts for something. Another test suggested that females mating with the peacocks with the most elaborate trains laid bigger clutches. It is also thought that the more eyespots a male has, the greater its mating success will be – but does this mean that the female stands in front of the displaying male going, 'one, two, three ...' before she mates with a male?

Yet another experiment suggests that the length of the fishtail feathers, combined with the number of calls a male gives, is another measurement of success. All this only goes to show that what might be universally well-known, is often not universally understood.

But there is no doubting this bird's astonishing effect on the world.

The famous train, of which the longest feathers are upper tail coverts, not the tail itself, is indeed an example of extravagance, with few equals anywhere in the avian world.

WEEK 28

Dark-necked tailorbird

Orthotomus atrogularis

SOUTHEAST ASIA AND ISLANDS

11–12cm (4½–4¾in)

 HERE'S SOME USEFUL ADVICE. IF YOU GO into a rural area in southern Asia, or even urban rough ground, you're going to hear a tailorbird singing. Recently I was on a birding trip and made several somewhat inept attempts at learning the sounds of the local avifauna. The trouble was that, almost every time I asked my guide what a hidden vocalist was, he very patiently repeated the response, 'Tailorbird, sir.'

These small birds, with their spiky bills and tails, are abundant undergrowth residents that usually remain concealed. Their vocal energy, though, is extraordinary; they are loud for such small birds, they are more than happy to sing all day and, if you are impressed by how a vocalist can summon up so many variations on the repetition of two or three notes, they have quite a wide repertoire. At any rate, they make a familiar backdrop to country life throughout the warmer parts of Asia.

There is a way of mastering the song, and that is to liken it to the sound of a sewing machine, or some other mechanical repetitive device – 'swit, swit, swit ...'. And if you do remember it this way, you are also connecting the sound with the type of behaviour that has made these small, plain, brown birds famous throughout the world. They are, genuinely, nature's sewing machines.

This is reflected in some of their local names. In Vietnam they are known as *chi chích bông*, the 'cotton warbler'; in Japanese the name translates as 'sewing bird'; and in Urdu *darza*, the 'tailoress'. All refer to a behaviour that is better developed in these species than in any other birds in the world.

They leave little to chance – after all, most tailorbirds nest during the monsoon, when heavy rain can damage their handiwork.

In the breeding season, tailorbirds stitch together two leaves, or the two sides of a single leaf, to make a pocket for their nest. Bearing in mind that this will contain their precious eggs and young, it's essential that the stitches do their job. In order to perform this marvel, the birds first have to choose living green leaves of the correct size, and they then use their long, slightly curved sharp bills – so well evolved for gleaning insects as part of the tailorbird's day job – to make holes in the outer perimeter of the leaves. Obviously, these mustn't be too close to the edge, or the leaves might tear.

Once they have perforated the leaves, the builders (they are always females) begin the stitching process. They weave any number of suitable materials, such as the fibres of plant down, silk from the cocoons of insects or cobwebs in through one hole, and then out through an opposing hole. They aren't able to knot the ends, so instead they fray them so that they are too wide to slip back through the hole. Thus, they staple the leaves together, stitch by stitch.

They leave little to chance – after all, most tailorbirds nest during the monsoon, when heavy rain can damage their handiwork. In most nests, there are about 150–200 strands stitched through the leaves, making the structure above, itself a quite intricate pouch of grasses and down, relatively sturdy. And, of course, just because there are eggs or young in the nest does not mean that the adult doesn't make repairs when necessary. Nevertheless, the sheer artistry and careful needlework required makes the nest one of nature's great marvels.

For the tailorbird, there are some advantages to being a bird that exists in close proximity to humanity. People are excellent at producing fibres. Urban tailorbirds often use processed cotton or wool instead of wild fibres, which are easy to find in villages and gardens. It's a clever piece of adaptation, assuring that singing tailorbirds of the future will still dominate the soundtrack of Asian scrubland.

WEEK 29

Black-naped oriole

Oriolus chinensis

EAST AND SOUTH-EAST ASIA

25–28cm (9–11in)

ONE OF THE GREAT TROPICAL EXPERIENCES that you can enjoy almost anywhere around the Equator is to enter a forest, particularly at dawn, and hear and enjoy a profusion of hidden voices. Unless you have specialist knowledge, or a guide to tell you what the birds are, this is a case of sweet immersion, taking in a new and thrilling atmosphere while remaining blissfully ignorant of the source of the sounds. Most tropical forests are so species-rich that it takes a lifetime to entangle the multifarious voices.

There are some tropical songsters, though, whose voices are instantly recognizable, even across the continents. One example is the oriole family (Oriolidae). They occur across the Old World (they don't occur in the Americas – the orioles there belong to a completely different family) and bring a dash of familiarity to the alien chorus. Most species sound much the same from Africa to Australia, and they all utter a rich, melodious fluting, which hopefully you can hear on this recording. These advertising calls are loud and far carrying. To my ear, their rich whistles, easily imitated, are absolutely redolent of tropical abundance.

Orioles do, though, carry a reputation for being notoriously difficult to see. They are desirable targets for birdwatchers because of the brilliance of their plumage, which usually sports a bright, buttery yellow – the name 'oriole' comes from the Latin *aureolus*, meaning 'golden'. However, they spend most of their time hidden in the canopy, where the foliage is densest, and they are restless birds, moving on quickly with a polished, undulating, fluent flight. They often fly a long way after gathering a few snacks from a tree, meaning that a bird you are straining to see one moment is suddenly far away, plucked from your grasp.

The orioles are medium-sized birds that combine a predilection for fruit with a strong stomach for formidable invertebrates. In one morning, they may switch from guzzling figs, a relatable delight, to gulping down hairy caterpillars. The hairs are often noxious and the body fluids the same, but the orioles seem unperturbed by the caterpillars' notoriety as they bash the larvae to a pulp on a nearby branch. Black-naped orioles have been observed breaking into wasps' or even hornets' nests to feed on the grubs within, so these are birds that are tough. They have also been seen raiding other birds' nests to eat eggs and nestlings. Their life in the canopy is no picnic.

Orioles build unusual homes. While most nests up in the trees rest on branches, that of the black-naped oriole is a cup suspended from two parallel branches, like a basket. The orioles are imaginative in their choice of material, which can include almost anything remotely vegetable in the vicinity, such as grasses, bark, straw, leaves and much more. The whole is bound together with cobwebs, another example of orioles giving the local invertebrates a hard time. The female builds the nest, but the male does bring in some material. Within the nest, the female lays 2–4 eggs.

The black-naped oriole is choosy about where it builds its nest, and one of the criteria it uses is the presence or absence of a neighbouring breeding pair of drongos (*Dicrurus* spp.). Drongos are famously noisy, attentive and aggressive, and have a completely fearless nature. Predators prefer not to be mobbed and attacked, so the area around a drongo's nest can be a relatively safe zone. There are many similar scenarios throughout the tropics – and indeed elsewhere – in which certain bad-tempered animals provide safe havens for other organisms. Some small birds deliberately nest near wasps' or ants' nests, for example. For orioles, drongos are the perfect neighbours from hell.

WEEK 30

House crow

Corvus splendens

MAINLY INDIAN SUBCONTINENT, INTRODUCED ELSEWHERE

40–45cm (16–17in)

SO FAR, EVERY WEEK OF THE YEAR IN THIS book has been devoted to a tropical songster that either thrills, delights or amazes. This week, though, I wish to introduce to you a character that nobody loves. Not all tropical birds are colourful or, indeed, tuneful. You only have to listen to the recording of the house crow's harsh caw to realize that.

The house crow is one of the overbearing personalities of southern Asia. You cannot easily get away from it, except in pristine forests and highlands. It is one of a select band of animals that is commensal with humankind, essentially only occurring where we are and nowhere else. It shares many of our attributes, including intelligence, curiosity and adaptability; it is also hyperabundant. And very, very noisy. Roosts of this bird, which form in the evening, descend into shouting matches, which are loud enough for a modest sized gathering – but some of these contain tens of thousands of birds.

You have to admire it, in many ways. What other bird would use bicycle pedals to line its nest? What other bird has been known to make a whole nest completely out of spectacle frames? These birds regularly eschew sticks for their cup-shaped nests, instead making them entirely out of wire, which they can bend into shape with their bills. They also regularly place these constructions on pylons, streetlamps and electricity poles, eschewing any notion of wildness. These are birds created by us.

Many of the world's crow species are known for their flexible diets, and the house crow is no exception. Many individuals feed on anything edible that they can find in the street, such as scraps and leftovers, carcasses and casualties. They are highly predatory, regularly catching rats and mice. Unfortunately, they are so fearless of people in many places that they will enter compounds and kill livestock. This boldness makes them very unpopular, as does their ability to raid crops of many kinds, but especially maize and sorghum, and to enter uninvited into storage facilities.

Everywhere they go, whatever the presiding climate, they seem to flourish as long as humans, with all their waste, are found.

Again, though, you have to admire these tenacious animals. House crows have been known to dive into water to catch fish, while they also sometimes attempt to catch flying insects, such as ants and termites, in mid-air. They are hopeless at this, but they keep trying, which is what house crows do. They also regularly ride on the backs of domestic grazers, such as cattle, doing them a service by eating their ticks, lice and flies, but at the same time doing some of them a disservice by biting at open wounds and stripping off flesh. They are regular visitors to beaches, markets and, in vast numbers, refuse tips.

And, dear reader, they are coming for you – that's if you're not reading this in India or neighbouring countries, where you already have the pleasure. House crows have made it to the Middle East onboard ships, and are already abundant in this very hot part of the world, and they are taking over. They have reached many places, often by the hand of humanity. Such places include ports and docks all around the Indian Ocean, including east Africa, Singapore and Hong Kong, China, as well as the Seychelles and Andaman Islands. Everywhere they go, whatever the presiding climate, they seem to flourish as long as humans, with all their waste, are found. Several populations in temperate areas, such as the Netherlands, have had to be eradicated. There are fears that they could easily colonize the Caribbean and North America.

Love it or loathe it, the house crow is a tropical bird on the move.

WEEK 31

Red-headed lovebird

Agapornis pullarius

CENTRAL AFRICA

13–15cm (5–6in)

WHEN IT COMES TO PUBLIC DISPLAYS OF affection, the lovebirds of Africa have caught the imagination of humanity. The scientific name *Agapornis* comes from the Ancient Greek *agape* (the highest, noblest form of love), while the typically stylish French name for these highly sociable mini parrots is *inséparables.* The birds earn their name by spending large amounts of time huddled together in bodily contact, or in mutual preening. They are monogamous over long periods of time. Unfortunately for the conservation of wild populations, lovebirds are widely kept in captivity, where this attractive aspect of their behaviour is particularly obvious.

You might think that Africa would be the natural home to dozens of species of parrots, but surprisingly the continent hosts only about 20 species, of which nine are lovebirds. Parrots truly flourish in South

America, Australasia and tropical Asia, somewhat bypassing the African continent. However, where they occur, the lovebirds are often quite common, with groups of them inhabiting grassy savannah and often flying over in moderate-sized flocks. Their calls are all high-pitched and somewhat insect-like screeches. Listen carefully to the recording of the red-headed lovebird, and perhaps you can imagine the sound of someone knocking some coins in their trouser pocket.

Popular and attractive they may be, but red-headed lovebirds, along with two other species, the black-winged (*A. taranta*) and black-collared lovebirds (*A. swindernianus*) are also notable for a strange and extraordinary behaviour that is unknown in any other bird – quite the party trick. These birds use holes for nesting, but add material and, quite extraordinarily, when they find a loose fragment of grass, they transport it by lodging it within their plumage. It seems incredible that they don't hold it in their bill, as most smaller birds do, or using their strong feet, like birds of prey.

The birds earn their name by spending large amounts of time huddled together in bodily contact, or in mutual preening.

But no, they metaphorically place it in their pocket, like a human shoplifter trying to sneak a pilfered item about their person. If there is a specific reason why they do this, nobody has figured it out, although presumably it means they can fly to the nest unimpaired, and it isn't obvious that they are bringing something in.

This isn't the only unusual aspect of the red-headed lovebird's breeding behaviour, because the nest-site itself is also unexpected. These birds almost always use an ant or termite nest for the hole, and generally one that is still occupied by its 'rightful' owners. It is thought that originally the holes would have been made by woodpeckers taking their fill of the insects, and they haven't been fully repaired. An ideal hole is 10cm (4in) in diameter and about 20cm (8in) deep, and the nest interior is often lined quite thickly with grass, and sometimes with excrement, presumably to discourage the inhabitants from wandering. These nests are usually found in trees 3–5m (10–16ft) above ground. These lovebirds lay 3–6 eggs, and the female incubates them for about three weeks. In keeping with the bird's romantic reputation, the male feeds her throughout this time, visiting several times a day.

These small parrots feed on the seeds of tall grasses, with a few occasional special treats such as figs. In order to digest this hard, dry food, red-faced lovebirds often ingest small stones and retain them in the stomach to help with digestion.

WEEK 32

'I'iwi

Drepanis coccinea

ISLANDS OF HAWAII

15cm (6in)

 SOME OF THE WORLD'S MOST GLORIOUS and remarkable birds are found on tropical islands. It isn't surprising. When animals or plants arrive in a new place, evolution has a party. The more isolated the location, the wilder the adaptations, the experiments and the wonder.

Something astonishing happened on the Hawaiian islands, shortly after they formed above the sea some 5.7 million years ago. A group of finches, not so different from those we know well from Europe and North America, arrived from eastern Asia. In a pristine land, far from any other (now more than 4000km (2500 miles) from a continent) they radiated into all kinds of forms, so diverse and colourful that they make the more famous Darwin's finches of the Galápagos Islands look stale and unimaginative. Often called the Hawaiian honeycreepers, they are the finished product of rampant evolution.

One of these is a stunning red bird called the 'i'iwi. The odd name comes from one of its contact calls. As you can hear from the recording, it has a perky song, although rather creaky and unstructured, like a slowed-down canary. The voice varies a great deal, and individuals often incorporate mimicry of other birds.

The illustration shows that the 'i'iwi is no longer anything like its finch-like ancestor, but over millions of years has evolved into a nectar specialist, with its sharply downcurved bill. The bill is ideal for probing into lobelias (*Clermontia*) and other plants with long, tubular corollas, the ones that are so famous for their associations with hummingbirds. When drinking nectar from these, it often hangs upside down to insert the bill. It is thought that the 'i'iwi and lobelias have coevolved over the centuries.

However, in the last 100 years, a change has occurred in the 'i'iwi's feeding. Remarkably, measurements of living 'i'iwis and old specimens have proven that 'i'iwi bills have shortened by 0.5cm (⅕in) over this time. This has probably happened because the native populations of lobelias have shrunk, and many species have become extinct. These days its primary foodplant is known locally as *ōhi'a* (*Metrosideros polymorpha*), an evergreen type of native myrtle that is, incidentally, the state flower of Hawaii, one with long, pom-pom like open flower clusters.

Many nectar-drinking birds will sometimes cheat by not inserting their bills into the flower, but instead puncturing a hole at the base of the corolla, an activity that bypasses pollinating the flower. This habit has become more frequent since the introduction of the supremely nectar-rich banana poka (*Passiflora tripartitia*), another significant change in the life of this bird.

You might have noticed that these changes in diet have not occurred randomly, but because of effects wrought by humans – the decline of native plants and the introduction of aliens. The shortening of the 'i'iwi's bill is a physical symbol of the destruction of Hawaii's native environment.

The story of Hawaiian honeycreepers began in style but, especially since human settlement, both by Polynesians and then Westerners, has greatly soured, with the honeycreepers withering on the vine. People ravaged Hawaii, cutting down forests and introducing a wide range of animals that killed or outcompeted the local fauna and flora. Catastrophically, mosquitoes were introduced, and these have become the scourge of Hawaiian honeycreeper, avian malaria causing the demise of many already vulnerable from loss and degradation of forests. About 20 species have become extinct, and most others, at least another 20, are on the way out. The 'i'iwi, found on most islands, is still common, but its future is unclear. Even now, it is confined to the mosquito-free zone above about 1250m (4100ft), but climate change means that mosquitos are creeping uphill as the uplands become warmer.

Enjoy this bird while you can.

The odd name comes from one of its contact calls. As you can hear from the recording, it has a perky song, although rather creaky and unstructured, like a slowed-down canary.

WEEK 33

Sparkling violetear

Colibri coruscans

THE ANDES, SOUTH AMERICA

13–14cm (5–5½in)

THE SPARKLING VIOLETEAR IS A HUMMINGBIRD found in the Andes. Who can write anything new about the wonders of hummingbirds? But this species, at least, can speak for itself. It is one of the most vocal of all, and this loud 'chit-chit ...!' is its song, which it repeats endlessly.

Many of the world's hummingbirds are quite restricted in distribution, sometimes just down to a few valleys, but this one is an exception. Not only does it occur along most of the Andean range, from Colombia down to Argentina, but it is also found from 1700m (5600ft) right up to 4500m (14800ft) in altitude. The higher levels are known as the páramo zone, a grassy, shrubby alpine habitat equivalent to the tundra. The sparkling violetear may breed here, exacting the great advantage of suffering very little predation, yet still drinking the abundant nectar in season. Some birds make altitudinal movements, moving down much lower after breeding, even to as low as 200m (660ft). More interestingly, though, some individuals make daily movements up and downhill. In the morning, they fly up to the páramo, but in the afternoon they retreat downwards to the edge of the forest.

In common with all hummingbirds, the sparkling violetear is a feathered miracle. Hummers have the highest heartbeat rate known among vertebrates. The resting rate of a human is 50–70 beats per minute, depending how fit you are, but that of a hummer is 500–600 per minute *at rest*. If it's flying fast, this rate may exceed 1000 beats a minute – it's exhausting just thinking about it.

Its breathing rate is also extraordinary: up to 500 breaths a minute when hovering. For such heavy aerobic exercise, powered by its nectar diet, the hummingbird needs to get oxygen around its system fast. Fortunately, its blood contains higher haemoglobin levels than any other animal measured to date.

> *Hummingbirds have an excellent memory for where good patches of blooms grow, but they also need acute vision. All birds have much better colour vision than humans.*

With a diet of 90 per cent nectar – most hummingbirds also eat small quantities of insects and spiders, sometimes catching the former in aerial sallies – every hummingbird in the wild needs access to copious flowers. Some individuals drink from about 2000 blooms a day. Hummingbirds have tubular, forked tongues, movable and very sensitive at the tip. They drink nectar by licking it up, about 13 times every second, and on average a hummingbird fills its crop in about four minutes, at which point it must pause and digest it, which takes about

15 minutes, so no hummingbird is active all the time. This, incidentally, is the fastest digestion time recorded for any vertebrate.

Although flowers stay still, they aren't everywhere and must be searched for. Hummingbirds have an excellent memory for where good patches of blooms grow, but they also need acute vision. All birds have much better colour vision than humans (birds have four types of colour-detecting cones, while we have three), and in the case of hummingbirds, this doesn't just help them to find the flowers, but assess them too. Colour cues, including those in the ultraviolet spectrum, betray how much nectar a flower bloom has, and the hummingbird's taste buds can detect the sugar content of the nectar. These birds really do have a battery of amazing skills.

In common with other hummingbirds, the sparkling violetear doesn't distribute breeding tasks fairly, and it is the female that carries out everything, from selecting a nest-site to building the structure, laying and incubating the eggs, and feeding the young (by regurgitation). The nest is a cup only 6cm (2¼in) in diameter, made up from grasses, which contains the two white eggs. The female incubates the eggs for 17 days and feeds the young for three weeks. How she finds the time for these tasks is just one more miracle in the lives of these awe-inspiring birds.

WEEK 34

Yellow-crowned gonolek

Laniarius barbarus

WEST AFRICA

25cm (9in)

 IF YOU LISTEN TO THE RECORDING HERE, you might not be particularly overwhelmed by the yellow-crowned gonolek's voice – it's just a rapid-fire rattle and a liquid note squeezed together, although, with imagination, it does explain the odd name 'gonolek'. There is, however, something extraordinary about it – it's uttered by two birds.

Almost any sound you hear from this lavishly coloured, skulking beauty will be a duet between a male and female. The two live together in close proximity all year long and between years – often for life. And the way they communicate is to blend their voices into a single song. If you listen, though, it doesn't seem possible that it's two birds, because the sounds are coordinated so perfectly.

Measurements have shown that the second bird responds to the first within a tenth of a second (0.08–0.1sec). Each motif, either the liquid 'pu' or the rasping call only lasts for a third of a second. To us, it's over before we could think of responding. The sequence often includes many repetitions (up to 40), with only a second between each, and these can go on almost throughout the day. It doesn't matter where each bird is, they still duet perfectly, even if they cannot see each other.

It's very much an equal effort, too. Although it's usually initiated by the male's 'pu' and the female rattling in kind, there are times when the female calls first and the male responds. Interestingly, though, in related species it was discovered that either bird has a same-sex tutor from which it learns its 'main' song. Each pair of gonoleks can sing several slightly different duets with slightly different notes, and after singing a sequence of one duet type, they will switch to another after a brief pause. Once a pair have established their repertoire, it remains the same for life.

But why do they duet like this, sometimes 1000 times a day? The answer is that it keeps the pair together and it keeps the territory intact. The family that the gonolek belongs to, the bush-shrikes (Malaconotidae) are renowned for their skulking behaviour, and it would be very easy for members of the pair to lose contact with one another, allowing unpaired birds of either gender to steal in and copulate with a bird that was temporarily separated – this happens a lot among birds. In terms of territory, it tells an intruding individual that the area is taken.

One of the curious things about gonoleks, and other members of the bush-shrike family, is that they are so gaudily coloured.

Sometimes interlopers do fancy their chances, and if this happens, they will attempt to duet with whichever sex is opposite. On such occasions, the incumbent male or female will quickly 'jam' the signal by calling in unison with its mate and the interloper, a vocal, but very brief *ménage-á-trois*. Usually, the trespasser quickly leaves.

After an intrusion, pairs of yellow-crowned gonoleks often enter into a particularly loud series of duets that rings across the dense bushes where they spend their lives. It is a kind of triumph ceremony.

One of the curious things about gonoleks, and other members of the bush-shrike family, is that they are so gaudily coloured. The sexes are alike and, as you can see from the illustration, they are a fabulous mix of black, scarlet and greenish golden yellow. For birds that spend much of their lives in the shade of dense foliage, gleaning for large invertebrates, it does seem surprising. But for us, when we observe them in the wild, they are a fabulous treat indeed.

WEEK 35

Golden bowerbird

Amblyornis newtoniana

NORTH-EAST AUSTRALIA

23–25cm (9–10in)

MALE BOWERBIRDS ARE FAMOUS THE world over for creating structures that they show to a visiting female, effectively saying, 'Look at my handiwork.' These structures, known as bowers, are not nests. They play no part in helping the female or young. They don't provide food or, quite honestly, do anything useful. Bowers are purely for decoration. They are the closest thing to bird art. A few other birds in the world make piles of stones and other items to make statements about themselves, but no other species comes close to creating such elaborate follies as bowerbirds.

   The golden bowerbird is a rare species found in highland forests in Queensland, Australia. About this time of year, after what is perhaps a heavenly break devoted mainly to guzzling fruit, the male returns to architectural design duties. This is the season that females may deign to visit, and the bower must look its best.

Anyone seeing a bower for the first time is struck by its size and intricacy, and that of the golden bowerbird is no exception. Its construction is known as a maypole bower (there are several other kinds), in which the bird collects sticks that it places around a sapling or branch to make a tower. There will be hundreds, if not thousands of these sticks, and they may be stacked up to 3m (10ft) high. Usually (in 64 per cent of examples), the bowers comprise two towers close together, and in this circumstance, with a stick running between these two 'massifs' that acts as the display perch. Typically, the sticks are piled in a highly haphazard fashion, and the overall impression is that this part conveys effort.

In order to build and maintain its bower, the male devotes inordinate effort to it. During the season (August–January), it is present for two-thirds of the daylight hours.

However high or broad the maypole bower is – and this varies enormously from bird to bird – the structure itself isn't enough, and the male owner spends much time decorating it, like a Christmas tree. The main decorations are greyish coloured lichens and flowers – and not just any flower, but specifically, creamy white ones. The site manager places its decorations close to where the display perch emerges from one of the towers.

In order to build and maintain its bower, the male devotes inordinate effort to it. During the season (August–January), it is present for two-thirds of the daylight hours, adding or modifying, making an average of 3.4 visits every hour, for 11 minutes each. A male may travel an average of 143m (470ft) to collect new material. One of the best ways to do this is to steal from a neighbouring bird's bower, and this happens a great deal!

Once a male has acquired a bower, which might take as long as five years, he will occupy it for many consecutive years, often until he dies. Bowers are often in traditional sites known to the local bowerbird population and have been known to be occupied for at least 20 consecutive years, and with a certain individual male for 16 years.

In a fair world, you'd think that a male's bower would be more than sufficient to impress any visiting female. After all, what better way to show its aptitude for breeding, its survivability and experience? But remarkably, since there will be other bowers in the area, a male must also show its fitness in other ways. It must sing for its supper and indulge in elaborate displays, none of which guarantee it the ultimate prize in copulating with its visitor.

No, it must sing an elaborate, inventive song, too. When you listen to the recording, you will be impressed by its sheer variety of loud whistles, squeaks and scolds, along with a remarkably loud rattling sound. It often incorporates much mimicry of other birds.

And it must perform a courtship display, including hovering, chasing and bowing – yes, bowing at a bower. Even then the female may not be entirely satisfied.

True, the female has much work to do, since she alone is responsible for all the breeding activities. And furthermore, she needs to make sure that she mates with the best possible set of genes for her offspring. But few female birds put potential mates through as many hoops as she does!

WEEK 36

Bay wren

Cantorchilus nigricapillus

CENTRAL AND NORTH-WESTERN SOUTH AMERICA

12–16cm (4¾–6¼in)

THE WRENS ARE FAMOUS FOR THEIR LOUD songs, many of which are also very complex. In the case of several species found in Central and South America, the songs are duets between a male and a female.

Listen to the recording, and you will struggle to hear that there are two birds. In this duetting species, unlike the yellow-crowned gonolek (see page 144), it is antiphonal, with one bird singing and then the other following so closely that you cannot easily tell. So, one unleashes a series of intricate, slightly slurred whistles, delightful in their clarity, and then the other effectively imitates it. Sometimes one bird adds in elements during the other's phrase, but the song is typically a pretty seamless combined effort.

The bay wren's singing has been well-studied, and it has revealed some surprising results. The first is that it is the female that begins the song, and the male that follows – again, this is different to the normal state of affairs in most duetting birds, in which it is often the male that starts. The second surprise is that bay wrens don't use their duets to defend territories, as many duettists do. Both male and female bay wrens can defend their own territories with their own songs; they don't need any help. Female song, either of a paired or unpaired bird, defends the territory from other females.

The males, meanwhile, use the duets to ascertain the quality of potential mates; presumably, if a female is on the ball acoustically, she is attractive. Once they have paired up, the male tends to join his mate in singing, sending a message to other males that she is taken. The duet is not to keep other males from the territory, but from the female.

The birds live in thickets, usually next to watercourses, but also occasionally alongside roads or tracks.

Despite the potentially cagey start, these pairs are often long-lasting, persisting throughout the year. The birds live in thickets, usually next to watercourses, but also occasionally alongside roads or tracks. Typically for wrens of most species, they are extremely skulking, making it difficult to get a view of them, despite their loud songs, which makes you think that the birds are just about to show themselves. They forage for a wide variety of invertebrates, using their long, curved bills to pick items off leaves and stems. Food items include spiders, bugs, earwigs, beetles and caterpillars.

The other claim to fame of the wren family is their nest-building ability. In many species the female partly selects the male on the quality of his constructions, but in this species, with song being the main bonding determinant, the two build the nest structure together. It is domed and quite large (it's been described as the size of a coconut), altogether about 25cm (10in) in length, with an entrance tunnel leading to a main section up to 13cm (5in) in diameter. It is made of various stems and leaves, sometimes with a little sprinkling of moss to decorate the outside. It is a pretty impressive piece of work.

The female lays 2–3 eggs. In quite a few members of the wren family, females have the unusual habit of destroying the eggs of other birds in other nests, apparently at random, for no reason that is yet understood. Whether the bay wren does this is unknown.

WEEK 37

Rhinoceros hornbill

Buceros rhinoceros

SOUTHEAST ASIA, ISLANDS OF SUMATRA, JAVA AND BORNEO

80–90cm (31½–35½in)

IT ONLY TAKES A GLANCE AT THE PICTURE here to imagine the sort of sound the rhinoceros hornbill would make. You'd be right, too. The loud honking is suitably resonant, and it carries a long way across the canopy of pristine lowland rainforests where this species occurs. Males and females frequently honk in duet, and they often give the impression that they could be a great deal noisier if they wanted to.

Hornbills occur throughout Africa and Asia, with most of the largest species occurring in the latter. The rhinoceros hornbill is one of the biggest, and in addition to the call it creates a swooshing noise as it flies, a sound that, in some species, can carry for 1km (⅔mile) or more. In contrast to most birds, the underwing coverts are poorly developed, and the noise is made by air rushing through the base of the large wing feathers. In the forest, you feel a tingle of anticipation as the noise of these great birds comes towards you as they fly above the canopy, with their deep wingbeats interspersed with glides. They are rainforest royalty.

The rhinoceros hornbill is named for its extraordinary casque, a strange ornamentation above the bill, which is built from the keratin covering the jaw. All hornbills have this hollow structure and, in most species, it is connected to the mouth and so probably contributes to the echoing quality of the calls. That of the rhinoceros hornbill is certainly one of the most impressive, with its shiny orange colouration and its unique upward (and sometimes slightly backward) tilt. You can imagine rival males locking horns, and they probably occasionally do in this species, as has been witnessed in others. The casque is undoubtedly a sexual ornament, in that males have bigger casques than females, and juveniles have undeveloped casques until they are at least a year old, and in larger species they may need six years to grow to full size. The colour may also vary, a powerful signal of individual quality.

Males and females frequently honk in duet, and they often give the impression that they could be a great deal noisier if they wanted to.

In common with many of the big, charismatic birds of tropical forests, hornbills are primarily consumers of fruit. The rhinoceros hornbill is especially fond of figs, as are many of its relatives, and may occasionally mix with others of its kind at a fruiting tree. In addition, the large, long, pointed bill enables it to catch a wide range of animals, from large invertebrates to lizards.

In the breeding season, hornbills exhibit a quite remarkable piece of behaviour, unique among all birds. When it's time to lay eggs, female hornbills find a large, natural cavity, often high up (to 15m (50ft)) in a tall forest tree, and then seal themselves in, leaving only a vertical slit. At first, they use mud collected from outside to fill in the hole, using the broad sides of their bill to lay it in bricklayer fashion, but for the final seal they use their own faeces and fragments of food, which are periodically brought in by the male. The slit-like shape of the entrance ensures some temperature regulation, with warm air rising from the female and her young replaced by cooler air sinking in from the entrance.

The female remains sealed for several weeks, although this is a choice, since she can easily break out, and does if the nest fails or when the young fledge. Most hornbills wait for some time before laying the first egg, and it may take a week or two before she completes the clutch. To cope with this interval, male hornbill sperm remains viable for an exceptionally long period of time, instead of just a few days as in most birds. The sealed female takes the opportunity to moult while incubating and brooding.

Throughout the nesting period, which amounts to up to 46 days of incubation and at least 40 days until fledging, the male spends its time finding food not only for itself, but also for its mate and brood (one or two young). He flies up to the nest hole and regurgitates what he has found. It is hard work, but the unusual arrangement ensures that the precious brood is safe from predators.

WEEK 38

Red-cheeked cordonbleu

Uraeginthus bengalus

SUB-SAHARAN AFRICA

12–13cm (4¾–5in)

 **THESE GEMS LIVE IN THE AFRICAN** savannah, often surrounded by famous megafauna. Sometimes they will forage on the ground within shadows cast by elephants or find themselves dislodged from the long grass by a warthog bathing in the dust. They are tinies in the land of the mighty.

You might wonder how such different animals coexist in the same place, but the cordonbleu's secret is a simple one. Its main diet consists of grass seeds, and grasses make savannahs. Grass seeds are superabundant, and they have many other qualities, too. They are long-lasting, which means that a small seed-eater can find them even in dry areas after many months. They are full of carbohydrates, up to 80 per cent by volume, so they are like high-energy snacks. And when broken down, one of the metabolites is water, allowing the birds to spend less time looking for water in what is a parched environment.

Most grass seeds are just a couple of millimetres in size, which also makes them easy to handle. In common with other seed-eaters, cordonbleus (which belong to a family of small birds called waxbills, Estrildidae) have a strong conical bill with sharp edges. This enables them to hold a seed in the palate and use the sharp edge to slice it open, and then move it with the tongue to de-husk, in the manner of an old-fashioned tin-opener.

Cordonbleus also feed on another, very different item of immense abundance in the African savannah – termites. These insects are everywhere, in the ground, in trees and within their own self-created mounds. Cordonbleus feed on the smallest species, often uncovering them by pecking the roof off their tunnels, fielding them as they come to investigate. Sometimes they will catch the flying versions of termites by snatching them in a short sally from the ground.

If you listen to the song on the recording, it is quite a complex, conversational twitter with many harsh, squeaky notes. Not surprisingly, cordonbleus have individually recognisable songs, suggesting that all or part of the song is learned. The female sings, too. Both male and female take part in defending their territory and the bond between them is a strong one. They spend a great deal of time in bodily contact and frequently preen one another.

Cordonbleus build quite substantial nests, about 10cm (4in) in diameter, ball–shaped and made from the stems and heads of grasses, sometimes with a few roots thrown on top. The interior is stuffed with soft materials, including many feathers, and sometimes these are placed strategically to hide the nest entrance. Inside the female lays 3–5 eggs. It's all done very rapidly. The nest is made and the eggs all laid within about a week. If they are feeling lazy, cordonbleus appropriate the old nests of various species of weaver, as do many forms of African wildlife, from snakes to insects.

The young of cordonbleus practise some highly unusual behaviour, unique among songbirds. Most nestlings, once they have hatched, beg loudly when their parents come to the nest with food, and stretch their necks up with great force, hoping to be first. The young of cordonbleus (and other waxbills) behave in a completely different manner. At first they are silent, and rather than stretching upwards, they keep their heads down, but twist them to the side so that the roof of their mouth points upwards and the tongue is lifted. They also move their heads, snakelike, from side to side.

Cordonbleus build quite substantial nests, about 10cm (4in) in diameter, ball-shaped and made from the stems and heads of grasses.

This strange behaviour enables the nestlings to show the parents the inside of their mouths, which is patterned with blue papillae and black spots. Every species in the family has a different pattern, and these unique mouths presumably help the parents to ensure that all their offspring are the 'right' species. Waxbills sometimes lay eggs in the nests of related species, and many are also parasitized by whydahs (see page 92).

WEEK 39

Andean cock-of-the-rock

Rupicola peruvianus

THE ANDES, SOUTH AMERICA

30–32cm (12–12½in)

GATHER ANY GROUP OF INTERNATIONAL birders together, and sooner or later they will devise a list of the world's top ornithological experiences – a bucket list for birdwatchers, if you will. Whenever that happens, you can be absolutely sure that one firm entry on everyone's list will be this: witnessing a cock-of-the-rock lek. The shenanigans of this species, and its close relative in northern South America, the Guianan cock-of-the-rock (*R. rupicola*), are simply among the most bizarre, wondrous and, actually, quite funny, of all avian gatherings.

Cocks-of-the-rock follow a breeding system known as lekking, in which males gather together to form a collective visual and aural display. The females visit the lek and decide which, if any, of the masculinity on the menu is worth their time. They may visit several leks to find that perfect specimen to inseminate them and contribute high value genetic material. The females perform all breeding duties, allying with males only for sex, so they don't mess about with poor-quality potential mates. The leks have a hierarchy in which the best birds display at certain parts of the lek, which is a self-sorting mechanism, guiding visiting females to the top bird. The other males – and there may be 15 altogether – simply observe while the chairman entertains the visitors. Occasionally a miracle occurs, and two females visit the dominant male at once: or they are distracted, or make a mistake, and a second-class male takes advantage. However, over the course of a season of several months, a single male monopolizes almost all the female attention.

> *They constantly bow down and flutter their wings to show off their grey coverts, and also jump about.*

Notwithstanding its ruthless meritocracy, for a detached human observer, the cock-of-the-rock lek is fantastic entertainment. As you can see from the illustration, the males have dashing, bright scarlet plumage, and a dandy-like crest. About the size of pigeons, they spend much of their time sitting on a perch some 4–6m (13–20ft) above the ground. They constantly bow down and flutter their wings to show off their grey coverts, and also jump about. All the time they make the extraordinary loud calls as heard in the recording, a sort of cross between the caw of a crow and the squawk of a parrot.

Wondrous though the spectacle is, I do hope I don't besmirch the reputation of this Andean montane icon by suggesting that it has a delicious amateurishness about it. The jumps and flutters are a little half-hearted, and the wild-eyed expression of the displaying males suggests that when they recover their poise, they might feel slightly embarrassed in retrospect. Compared to the admittedly peerless manakins, with their professional-looking dance routines, this is more like dad-dancing. Let's hope the female cocks-of-the-rock don't think so.

There is one additional extraordinary aspect to the lek displays, however. If you watch carefully, you will see that the heart of the performance is a challenge and threat towards another bird on the same or different branch. This is intentional and coordinated, because the males act in pairs. They bow to each other, on all parts of the lek. Duos of males are in it for the long haul; they display together throughout the season and perhaps subsequently. When they feed, they often go off together.

When a female visits, however, it is, quite naturally, every male for himself. Although the duos display together in the presence of the female, the lek hierarchy doesn't change – only one male gets to copulate. The other male, the colleague, looks on, presumably not knowing where to put its eyes. Why on earth, though, would any male put itself through mutual display with only one winner? Nobody is entirely sure, but perhaps the 'spare part' male eventually inherits the top bird's crown?

The mystery simply underlines how marvellous and complicated some tropical birds are.

WEEK 40

Common hill myna

Gracula religiosa

INDIA AND SOUTHEAST ASIA

25–35cm (10–13¾in)

IS IT POSSIBLE FOR A TROPICAL BIRD TO have too good a voice? In the sorry case of the common hill myna, the answer would have to be yes. This bird has a stunningly clear and varied voice, and at dawn its utterances ring out from the forest canopy in a delightful cacophony. It makes gurgling sounds, screeches, croaks and wails, bell-like sounds and several marvellous descending whistles, like the second half of a wolf-whistle. These sounds have a remarkable dynamic and frequency range, from quiet whispers to piercing blasts, and from high-pitched shrieks that seem to go through you, to lower sounds approaching that of human speech. Several of these birds singing at once is like listening to a classic concert of electronic music.

Sometime in the distant past, people must have swapped catching and eating hill mynas, which are quite large and make a decent helping of curry, to keeping them as pets. Some time later, they made a remarkable discovery: the hill myna can mimic human speech almost perfectly. For centuries, this gift has made the myna one of the most coveted of all cagebirds, and its fame has spread all over the world. Millions of mynas live a life behind bars. At worst, their vocal prowess shrinks to a few odd calls, plus imitations of humans saying stupid things, all for entertainment.

Mynas also eat a wide variety of other animals, including insects. For relatively large birds, they are surprisingly good at snapping up insects in flight.

It is just as well the common hill myna has a widespread distribution, which includes many protected areas and vast forests. If not, it would be severely threatened with extinction in the wild. But it is vulnerable almost everywhere it occurs and, worse still, it is the chicks in the nest that are taken, these being the ones that can be trained to 'talk'. In many countries trapping is banned, but the temptation is too great for some impoverished people. In various parts of the world, the birds are encouraged to use artificial nest boxes fairly low to the ground – this bird usually nests high up – so the young can be taken.

Cages are a far cry from the abundance of the hill myna's wild habitat. It tends to occur in tall, lush, humid forests, with lofty perches for its singing, feeding and pairing. It usually occurs in hilly areas between 300m (1000ft) and 2000m (6600ft). Up in the canopy, it feeds on a wide variety of items, with fruit being a particular favourite and figs above all, as is the case for many tropical birds, especially in Asia. Fruits below 20cm (8in) in diameter it plucks and eats whole, while larger fruits are bitten. In common with other members of the starling family (Sturnidae), it seems to bolt its food, and it has a distensible stomach for storage, allowing it to gather much at one sitting.

One of the items that appears a little unexpectedly on the myna's menu is reptiles, particularly lizards and geckoes. These can be up to 30cm (12in) long – another challenge to that gullet. These are apparently especially prized, and a bird that has seized one is often chased by other birds, hoping to steal it. Mynas also eat a wide variety of other animals, including insects. For relatively large birds, they are surprisingly good at snapping up insects in flight.

These birds pair for life and in a good season they may raise three broods of 2–5 young. Theirs is a rich life, so long as they are left alone.

WEEK 41

Yellow-vented bulbul

Pycnonotus goiavier

SOUTHEAST ASIA AND ISLANDS, INCLUDING THE PHILIPPINES

19–20cm (7½in–8in)

DO YOU HAVE A CHEERFUL FRIEND whose ebullience begins to grate at times, if ever so slightly? This might just sum up humanity's relationship with a delightful and life-affirming family of birds, the bulbuls (Pycnonotidae).

What you can hear on the recording is a song that is repeated, with variations, throughout almost the whole of Africa, the Middle East and Asia, including many offshore islands. It is, in a way, a universal sound of the Old World tropics. An engineer could record almost any bulbul and use it as a wild soundtrack to convey a garden or forest. Bulbuls and their songs are everywhere, from the depths of African jungles where people never go, to gardens in enormous, sprawling Asian cities. Most of the 120 or so species have a distinct family signature, the cheerful, jaunty, slightly bubbling song, a song that's on repeat all day, every day, from dawn to dusk. The song is joyful – there is even a bulbul called the joyful greenbul (*Chlorocichla laetissima*) – but also an earworm. The celebrated author and ornithologist Reginald Ernst Moreau described one species as 'liable to indulge in wearisome iteration'.

Anybody from an Asian Islamic society will know about bulbuls, though. It is a word, and a bird, of huge cultural significance. An accomplished musician is often called a bulbul, and there is an Indian musical instrument called a 'bulbul tarang'. Bulbuls are part of a rich folklore, a mainstay of epic poetry associated with love.

Except, they aren't. This is a case of mistaken identity. The bulbul in the epic poems is actually a nightingale (*Luscinia megarhynchos*), the same bird that is lauded in Western culture. For some reason, the name bulbul came to be associated with the noisy garden birds instead of the skulking migrant with the angelic voice, and because bulbuls are so common, the name stuck and the confusion, steeped in the past, is now destined to go on into the future.

It is primarily a fruit-eater and will take any kind of fruit, nut or berry, and this includes many types of introduced garden plant.

The yellow-vented bulbul is one of the most abundant Asian species. It is a medium-sized songbird with a strong bill and a reasonably long tail. The plumage is fairly soft, and the scientific name of the family, Pycnonotidae, means 'dense-backed', here referring to the feathering. In common with most of the family, it is modest in colouration, apart from the obvious white stripe over its eye and its eponymous patch of yellow under the tail.

This particular species is remarkable for its extraordinary adaptability, with a very broad diet and an ability to turn its beak to almost any niche. It is primarily a fruit-eater and will take any kind of fruit, nut or berry, and this includes many types of introduced garden plant. It is also expert at catching insects, not only picking them from leaves or bark (a very 'bulbul-esque' method) but also catching them in mid-air sallies. It easily takes to another common tropical technique, that of stealing nectar from flowers, often piercing them at the base of the corolla, rather than bothering to enter the bloom. Somewhat surprisingly, it will also take carrion, which few other bulbuls do. It is undoubtedly one of the most successful of its kind. It is one of the few species that has adapted well to the growth of oil-palm plantations in Asia.

With such a broad range of skills and tastes, this is one tropical bird that is thriving. Its outlook, you might say, is joyful.

WEEK 42

Greater bird-of-paradise

Paradisaea apoda

NEW GUINEA

FEMALE 35cm (13¾in), MALE 43cm (17in)

THERE PROBABLY ISN'T A SINGLE READER of this book who wouldn't want the chance to follow in the footsteps of the person who made this recording. Who would not want an audience with a bird-of-paradise? As well as the opportunity to go to New Guinea? Famed the world over for their extraordinary opulent plumage – they have a greater variety of feather shapes than any other bird family in the world, despite numbering only 44 species – and their dazzling displays, the birds-of-paradise are among the most famous and celebrated birds in the world, and rightly so.

If you believe in a heaven, or a paradise, you might fully expect the birds you meet there to look like this – lavish, extravagant, colourful and vivid. But the origin of the family's name is intriguing. The first skins to reach bird enthusiasts in the 16th and 17th centuries were at first considered fakes, composites of different birds put together for fraudulent profit. But soon, so many reached Europe that they realized they were genuine. Stoked by awe, and in the knowledge that the Malays already called them 'birds of the gods', those early naturalists described how these beauties were birds of the ether, never coming down to earth. But this was a misconception fuelled by the habit of traders of cutting off the feet of dead specimens, and often their wings too, to make them easier to handle (the greater bird-of-paradise's scientific name *apoda* means 'no feet'). But the name stuck anyway.

It is satisfying to report that, in their native land, birds-of-paradise have never been taken for granted, even by those who wandered into the highland forests and saw them day by day. They are still revered. Their feathers have been traded between parts of New Guinea and the nearby islands since time immemorial, and plumes have been used in rituals, ceremonies and dances for at least 10,000 years. The plumes still find their way into head-dresses, which continue to be used in important social functions. Many dances in the catalogue of the unfathomably complex cultures of the multi-ethnic melting pot that is the Papuan Highlands, are based on the displays of birds-of-paradise.

The greater bird-of-paradise is the subject of some of these performances. It is a classically lavish example of the species, with a relatively normal front part – albeit with a blue bill, shining green throat and buttery yellow nape – and a back part dominated by flank plumes that explode out from under the wings to resemble a frozen waterfall descending from the bird's body. The plumes are apricot-yellow at the base, but white at the tip. When the bird is displaying, the plumes are erect and shaken, as if the birds is really a firework that has just been lit.

As if the sight of the ignited plumes wasn't enough, the male performs several moves to display to even better advantage. He spreads his wings and crouches on a perch or, to make it truly different, he will hang upside down, also with spread wings, so that the plumes drape over his head. All the time he will call loudly, his cries echoing through the treetops. In the final precopulatory display, he envelops the female with his wings.

You'd think that any female would fall for that, but of course, the male's marvellous display takes place in a marketplace. Indeed, in this species, up to 15 males all display close together in a single treetop: all call and shimmy every plume they have. The female makes her choice, copulates with the best one, and then goes on to build a nest (out of epiphytic orchid fronds, no less, among other material) and raise the family entirely by herself.

There are forests in New Guinea where ten or more species of these extraordinary birds occur together, all with their mindboggling displays. It is, for a birdwatcher, paradise indeed.

WEEK 43

Village weaver

Ploceus cucullatus

SUB-SAHARAN AFRICA

17cm (6¾in)

THERE ARE FEW MORE VIVACIOUS BIRDS in Africa than the weavers. Theirs is a hustle and bustle of existence, a noisiness, a busy-ness, one throbbing with activity. Many species live in colonies and carry out their day-to-day lives communally. They won't win prizes for their beautiful voices, but it doesn't matter, you are going to hear them anyway. Their harsh chatters and buzzes are part of the aural fabric of rural African life.

Weavers are famed for their nests, which you see everywhere hanging from trees and bushes. They are usually globular masses of interwoven grass fibres, which from a distance resemble very large, dried-out fruits. There are often a number of nests in a given tree, up to 200 in a large one, at least in the case of the present species, which is one of the most widespread and common in Africa.

The reproductive life of the village weaver revolves around the nest, which is built by the male. These birds have a special talent for stitching fibres together, very much analogous to human weaving, and it is largely the skill of the male's weaving that determines its success in pair formation. During the breeding season, about this time of year in most places, males are busily building up their body of work, and pairing up is rather like a property viewing.

Weavers are justifiably famous for these nests, because they uniquely involve intricate stitching. Plant fibres may be interlaced at right angles and passed through others to make a latticework. Fibres are also looped around supports and within the general structure. This is all done by no other method than pulling and pushing with the bill; the bird isn't able to make a knot, but uses the friction caused by looping.

To start a nest, a bird weaves fibres to make a bridge between two supporting twigs. It then usually weaves a ring below the bridge, which it gradually thickens by adding more and more thatching. Soon it can perch on the lower part of the ring, and it proceeds by adding more and more concentric rings. Eventually, the rings reduce in diameter to leave a globular nest. A male makes the roof waterproof by adding broader grass stems or other leaves. The last part is to remember to leave an entrance hole at the bottom! The entrance is at the bottom of a short tubular extension facing downwards.

As mentioned above, these nests aren't only potential homes for a brood of eggs and chicks, they are also the male's calling card. In village weaver life, every male has a small territory on the branch of a tree and builds as many nests as he can; he will often start the process before the breeding season actually begins. Every nest – and a male might build 20 in a season of a few months – has the potential to attract a mate, the more the merrier. A highly successful male might be the landlord for as many as five females all breeding at the same time. Its nests may be only 10cm (4in) apart.

When a female enters his territory, then, the male embarks on some noisy nest-invitation calling, and hangs upside down on the nest entrance, fluttering his wings rapidly to show his yellow underside. In the crowded colony, all the neighbouring males do the same, and competition is intense. Once a female enters the nest, the male sings loudly outside. The female may take as many as 20 minutes to decide yes or no. If a female rejects the nest, the male may rapidly tear it up and try building another.

In village weaver life, every male has a small territory on the branch of a tree and builds as many nests as he can.

Females select their mates based on the number of his nest-invitation displays, and of course on his ability to build a nest. She may also seek out a male with whom she has paired up before. If a female likes the nest, she will line it with soft grass and eventually lay 1–5 eggs.

It's a harsh world in a village weaver colony; many males fail to attract any females at all. Their hard work isn't always rewarded.

WEEK 44

Jungle babbler

Argya striata

INDIAN SUB-CONTINENT

25cm (10in)

THE LOCAL NAME FOR THE JUNGLE babbler, a very common and familiar sight in India, is *saat bhai*, which means 'seven brothers' in Hindi. It's a delightfully apt name for a group-living species, although not strictly correct. If there are seven birds, one will be an adult male, one an adult female, and the rest will actually be siblings, all offspring of the adults. But it's pretty close.

The jungle babbler's social arrangements, long-term membership of a family flock, are common in the tropics and warmer regions of the world, but rare in temperate areas. The long-tailed tit (*Aegithalos caudatus*) is an exception from northern Europe. Temperate breeding birds often have shorter lifespans than tropical birds and can less afford to wait for breeding opportunities. In the case of jungle babblers, youngsters don't leave the flock until their second summer, more than a year after hatching.

Babbler flocks are often very noisy, and if you listen to the recording, you will hear a cacophony of laughing, grating calls, which are typical, especially after excitement, such as a territorial bicker with the family next door. Detailed studies have shown that each bird has a vocabulary of 15 different calls, reflecting alarm, contact, flight-intention and many others, which help coordinate the whole. They are seldom silent, even at the roost site.

Membership of the flock puts responsibilities on the grown-up fledglings remaining with their parents. When they are feeding (mainly on ground invertebrates such as beetles and grasshoppers, but also frogs, with some vegetable matter too) especially as they spread from dense cover over open ground, all members of the flock take their turn as sentries, giving loud alarm calls in case of danger. The need for vigilance means that each member takes it in turns, their stint lasting an average of less than four minutes in the morning, but up to ten in the afternoon. Normally, a sentinel calls time on its own session by giving a special call, but on other occasions it hops down from its post to feed, and another replaces it. A study found that, for 82 per cent of the time, a sentinel was on duty.

Detailed studies have shown that each bird has a vocabulary of 15 different calls.

The juvenile flock members are also required to help with the adults' nesting attempt. In this species, these duties include bringing nesting material to the site, as if they had paid a visit to the DIY store; this is an unusual extra task not often seen among helpers. They also play a pivotal role in the rest of the breeding attempt, bringing in their own food offerings to the nestlings and fledglings – in other words, feeding their younger brothers and sisters. It is a whole family operation.

It isn't all work though. In the heat of the day, the whole group indulges in what is known as 'clumping', in which the birds sit so close together on a perch that they make physical contact. Clumping is contagious, so that flock members tend to pile in when clumping has begun. Clumped birds invariably indulge in allopreening, in which one bird preens the other, often in those hard-to-get-at places such as around the neck and throat. In larger flocks, subordinate birds clump and allopreen in order to curry favour with senior members of the flock.

In the non-breeding season, family flocks often amalgamate, so that it is quite possible to see groups of up to 20 birds. This allows the opportunity for young birds to change flocks if they wish. Apparently, young females need to leave in order to breed, while young males sometimes stay to inherit the territory. However, the group structure is so successful that survival is about 90 per cent per annum, great for the species but not so good for birds aspiring to branch out. Patience would seem to be the best strategy.

WEEK 45

White-browed robin-chat

Cossypha heuglini

CENTRAL AFRICA

19–20cm (7½–8in)

THIS ISN'T A BAD BIRD SONG TO HEAR IN your garden, is it? What a delightful virtuoso performance of confidence and perfect diction. You can hear that the singer repeats a phrase several times before progressing on to the next, and everything sounds practised and polished.

I have been fortunate enough to see and hear this species singing on a rooftop of a house in Entebbe, Uganda, at about this time of year. It was early in the morning, and without warning a pair of white-browed robin-chats faced each other on the top tiles, flicked their tails rhythmically from side to side, thrust their heads back and sang lustily. A few seconds later a neighbouring pair responded in kind, the robin-chat dawn declaration. It didn't last long, but the point was made.

Usually, only the male of this species sings, but as the sun rises, the pair performs a duet. The male takes the main part and the female adds a 'tsee' note at the end of the male's section. Pairs also duet during day if other pairs are in combative mode, perhaps challenging over territory. Robin-chats are among the many tropical birds that duet, far more than in the temperate zones, from which most birdwatchers hail. In the tropics, females sing a great deal more anyway, and in a few species they sing more than the males.

The male and female live in a shared territory long term, staying together throughout the year.

The white-browed robin-chat is a bumptious species. If an individual is feeding on an open patch of ground, perhaps a lawn, and becomes disturbed, it won't hesitate to attack another bird, even of a different species. This is because it feeds on the ground on invertebrates that might be flushed out of reach by other feeders nearby, so it doesn't tolerate them.

It is equally intolerant of threats and is well known for its fortitude when faced with potential predators such as snakes. When it finds one it gives off loud, rattling calls and will mock-peck at the predator's head, not usually daring to make contact. There is, though, a record of a robin-chat actually striking a large individual of one of Africa's deadliest serpents, the boomslang (*Dispholidus typus*) and almost dislodging it from a branch above the ground. Strangely, when mobbing predators, the robin-chat will suddenly show off a talent for mimicry of other birds, especially their alarm calls. Rather than incorporating these into its territorial song, it uses them in its quiet subsong; perhaps it does this to suggest that many species of birds are mobbing the predator.

If all is quiet, the white-browed robin-chat feeds in a style reminiscent of blackbirds (*Turdus merula*) and other thrushes in Europe and North America. It makes long, two-footed hops across the leaf litter, then stops perhaps to sweep away surface foliage, before hopping further along. It uses its hearing to detect food close to the ground, and in this simple way it can eat all kinds of invertebrates, such as ants (a particular favourite) and beetles.

The male and female live in a shared territory long term, staying together throughout the year. In the breeding season, the female constructs a substantial cup of leaves and twigs, which it places above ground, usually in a tree stump. She lays 2–3 eggs and, in a good season, may be able to bring up two clutches.

WEEK 46

Toco toucan

Ramphastos toco

SOUTH AMERICA

55–65cm (21½–25½in)

 YOU CAN SPEND HOURS WATCHING toucans before anybody asks the obvious question. Earlier this year I spent a few days at a jungle lodge in Costa Rica, where all day toucans of various sorts would come to the feeders in front of the restaurant, while the people drank beer and coffee. People would watch and take endless photographs, they would talk about what species of birds had visited, and they would chat about world affairs. But it was many hours before anyone said:

'Why does the toucan have such a big bill?'

This is, if you like, the toucan question. If ever there was a group of birds that symbolized the American tropics, other than hummingbirds, it would have to be these oddly top-heavy looking characters, who fly over the canopy with a weak-looking, undulating flight (apparently some large toucans struggle to cross big Amazonian rivers). Not only is the bill large, but it is also colourful and boldly patterned. There is no other group of birds whose bills could so well inspire the designs of carpets, tiles or plates, for example. And in parts of South America, they do.

These patterns on the toucan's bill, though, are something of a mystery. Such a large and bold part of a bird is usually a symbol of sexual selection, as in the case of a peacock's tail (see page 116). But surprisingly, the bills of male and female toucans are the same, so unless some very subtle differences are important, this seems not to be the answer. A striking livery could also help toucans differentiate between species, preventing hybridisation. Yet some species have variable bills anyway and freely interbreed, so this isn't it, either.

The only hypothesis remaining, in terms of pattern, is that the striking bill makes a toucan intimidating. Being primarily fruit-eaters, toucans have a lot of competition in the forest canopy, and if they can shoo away other frugivores with very little effort, it works to their advantage.

Of course, having a large bill would have the same effect, but the size and shape confers other advantages, too. The beak is astonishingly light, comprised mainly of keratin and a lot of empty space, with small struts holding the structure together. Take a closer look, and you will see that the bill has a slightly hooked tip and forward-facing serrations. These are all excellent adaptations for grabbing. And if you watch a toucan in the canopy, as opposed to one coming to bananas at bird feeders, it all suddenly makes sense. When a toucan is up in the treetops, it is forever reaching forwards, grabbing fruits from thin branches. It is acrobatic for a large bird, quite content to hang upside down at times – whatever enables it to reach those hard-to-get-at morsels. With a long bill, you have a long reach, and that seems to be that.

This ability allows the toucan to add some unusual items to its diet.

Although fruit is crucial, toucans aren't vegetarians. They also use their bill to tear the nests of other birds, and to eat the eggs and nestlings contained within. Toucans in aviaries often eat birds that intrude into their space, and tropical scientists using mist nets to catch birds often have to deal with marauding toucans coming down for an easy meal. Although many tropical fruit-eating birds eat little else, it seems that toucans require the extra protein.

The beak is astonishingly light, comprised mainly of keratin and a lot of empty space.

There are some secondary purposes to the bill, too. Some toucans fence each other during territorial skirmishes. The beak surface also allows the bird to lose heat from the body – birds don't have sweat glands, so they need to cool down in other ways. Fortunately, it seems that the bill doesn't add an echo chamber to the toucan's unmusical grunts.

No, it's all about grabbing.

WEEK 47

Wompoo fruit-dove

Ptilinopus magnificus

NEW GUINEA AND AUSTRALIA

29–45cm (11½–17¾in)

IN MANY PARTS OF THE WORLD, PIGEONS and doves are humanity's neighbours. From rock pigeons (*Columba livia*) in urban centres worldwide, to a plethora of doves cooing dirges in suburbia, they are so ubiquitous that we tend not to admire them much. But, away from our settlements, pigeons and doves (there is no technical difference between the two) blossom into some of the most glorious birds anywhere. In tropical forests and on faraway islands, they gleam with bright colours and utter delectable phrases. In all, there are 350 species, but they are birds of a thousand hues and coos.

Take just one example, the wompoo fruit-dove, a tropical forest species found in New Guinea and Australia. Just look at those colours, from the lush green on the upperparts, to the rich, deep purple on the breast and the hidden but vivid mustard-yellow under the tail. This is a glorious bird; even the grey head looks as though it has just been painted on. Yet I have chosen this species to represent forest pigeons because of its delightful advertising call. The epithetic 'wom-poo' has a delicious air of pomposity, as many pigeon sounds do; it makes me laugh.

Pigeons (Columbidae) are a fabulously successful bird family, partly because they do many things very well indeed. They have strong legs for perching and their muscular wing muscles, which may account for 40 per cent of their total weight, allow them to take off almost vertically, and fly swiftly. They are among the few birds that can suck water directly without lifting up their heads, and this enables them to drink from tiny puddles on branches, or take drops off leaves.

The pigeon family's most surprising gift, though, is that its members feed their chicks in a supremely efficient way. They don't bring in whole foods, neither do their regurgitate food. Instead they process vegetable matter within the crop and repurpose it as a kind of 'milk,' albeit a rather solid, curd-like substance that forms in the epithelial cells. This is extremely nutritious and allows the pigeon young (squabs) to grow rapidly. Many pigeons lay two eggs, but the wompoo fruit-dove only lays one.

The family is notorious for their flimsy nests, which are merely platforms on branches, often high above ground. This fruit-dove builds a better effort than most, although the egg can still often be seen from

It is surprisingly agile up in the branches and is perfectly capable of hanging upside down on the ends of branches if need be.

below. The nest does look somewhat small for the size of bird, too, just 15cm (6in) in diameter. The female often builds it in a day but then, somewhat strangely, may not lay an egg in it for six weeks.

But what all pigeons do well is eat. This species, as its English common name suggests, mostly eats fruit. Once it has found a source, it tends to stay with it, remaining on a laden tree for the whole day if it isn't disturbed. It is surprisingly agile up in the branches and is perfectly capable of hanging upside down on the ends of branches if need be, especially to get at berries. It can also dexterously walk along boughs. One way to see one of these beauties is to listen for the sound of falling fruit.

Just because they are fruit specialists doesn't make this pigeon's diet dull. A study in New Guinea found that the wompoo fruit-dove ate more than 50 species of fruit. In a sense it is a bon viveur, living the high life, with everything it needs.

WEEK 48

Common potoo

Nyctibius griseus

CENTRAL AND SOUTH AMERICA

35–38cm (15–15in)

 **IF YOU THINK THAT OWLS MAKE THE** eeriest, most peculiar night sounds among birds, you've obviously never heard the cry of a common potoo. If you listen to this recording, you may well find that your credulity is stretched, that you can only just believe this is a real bird.

Many nocturnal forest species evoke fear with their disembodied calls, but the common potoo's loud, self-pitying lamentation, evidently becoming more and more despairing as it steadily drops in pitch, is perhaps too relatable to stir terrors. We have all had days at whose end these huge sighs might just be echoed. In Trinidad, the dirge is rendered 'poor me, one', and in Brazil, where the potoo is sometimes called *urutau*, it is thought to represent the souls of those who have lost lovers or are forever unrequited.

Another Brazilian name is *mãe-da-lua*, meaning 'mother of the moon', a deliciously evocative epithet that has a strong basis in fact. Apparently, potoos are stimulated to call by moonlight. They vocalize most strongly around the time of the full moon and may in fact call all night at this time, whereas in complete darkness they are much quieter.

Potoos are very odd birds, closely related to another nocturnal family, the nightjars (Caprimulgidae), which also catch flying insects at night, but they are larger and, when perching, they sit upright. During the day this helps them blend in with branches to such an extent that they are almost impossible to see; they simply look like a broken-off stump. They are also able to stay almost completely still for long periods of time.

They are insect-grabbing and gobbling machines. The head is large and the mouth broad and capacious, with a tiny bill that nonetheless bears a small projection like a tooth, which might help kill prey. Unlike nightjars, they lack bristles around the mouth. The eyes are absolutely enormous, and placed on the side of the head so that their all-round vision is excellent. If you spotlight a potoo in the forest at night, the eyes reflect back red. During the hours of darkness these birds really come alive, sitting upright on perches waiting for a large insect, such as a moth or a beetle, to come within range. If it does, the potoo flies off, using its long wings and tail for excellent manoeuvrability.

Although potoos eat a lot of moths – and the tropical forest is usually overflowing with them – they also eat a wide variety of other insects that are well armed, including mantises, beetles and cicadas. Potoos have rather delicate bills, but the inside of the mouth is strongly muscular, and potoos generally just swallow what they catch, apparently without fuss. The life they lead is not especially taxing or open to wild adaptation, and it is interesting to note that potoos have quite extraordinarily small brains, about the same size as that of a hummingbird. It looks like a short plank, and is evidently as thick as two of them!

Their imagination doesn't extend much to nesting, either. The birds select a depression in a branch, usually one pointing upwards at an angle, and simply lay their egg in it. The egg is often visible from the ground, and bearing in mind this can be 20m (66ft) above ground, this seems quite risky. Fortunately, they only lay one, and both sexes take turns to incubate it. The young potoo hatches covered in pale down and, if it were possible, looks even more like a part of a branch than the adult.

WEEK 49

Buff-breasted paradise kingfisher

Tanysiptera sylvia
NEW GUINEA AND NORTHERN AUSTRALIA
29–37cm (11½–14½in)

FORGET EVERYTHING YOU THOUGHT YOU knew about kingfishers. This one is completely different. For a start, it doesn't eat fish. Australians will be aware that their other famous kingfisher, the laughing kookaburra (*Dacelo novaeguineae*) doesn't either, but most other kingfishers in the world do. It doesn't dive into water, either.

Instead, the paradise kingfisher spends some of its time doing the complete opposite, making sallies into the vegetation to catch insects, upwards or sideways. More often, though, it perches low to the ground, dropping down on to a wide variety of prey, including snails, centipedes, spiders, worms and capacious insects, such as beetles, wasps, ants and even mantises. It sometimes digs for worms, which is also not a very kingfisher-like thing to do.

At this time of the year, buff-breasted paradise kingfishers are arriving in northern Australia from their wintering grounds in New Guinea. This species is, then, a good example of an intra-tropical migrant. Most readers will be most familiar with the temperate to tropical shifts of long-distance northern hemisphere summer migrants, but there are dozens of examples around the world of all sorts of birds moving within the tropical zone. This one is a good example. In fact, curiously, many individuals of the same species remain in New Guinea all year round. Migrants, meanwhile, occupy their own exclusive territories on their wintering grounds, presumably alongside their stay-at-home peers. They return to New Guinea in March and April.

The pair does take it in turns to incubate the eggs, of which there are usually three, but the female always takes the night shift.

During their migration, which takes them 150km (93 miles) over the Torres Strait, perhaps in a single flight, these birds fly in flocks. That would have to be a wondrous sight, with these colourful birds flying high, looking like huge butterflies with their pure white tail-streamers, some 20cm (8in) long, trailing behind, and using fluent wingbeats. In the Australian spring, the birds have a habit of arriving very suddenly, the waterside forests suddenly resounding overnight to their slightly gruff, tittering calls.

All members of the kingfisher family nest in holes that they excavate themselves, but of course, the buff-breasted paradise kingfisher has to be a bit different and edgy, doesn't it? Its holes are made in the side of a termitarium, a feature that dots the landscapes of northern Australia. Never mind that the termites are still at home; this doesn't seem to bother the new residents at all. The termites presumably just sigh deeply and put up with them. At the end of the season the colonial insects simply seal the tunnel up.

Both sexes dig the burrow, but their enthusiasm for the task is slightly different. Both use their feet and bill, but the female also uses its long tail to sweep debris away from the burrow as she goes. The male, on the other hand, which has a longer tail, holds its tail up and doesn't use it for sweeping. Presumably the tail is a statement of fitness, and the male does not want it damaged. The tunnel ends up being up to 20cm (8in) long, ending in a nest-chamber. In common with many kingfishers, nest sanitation is non-existent, and the chamber soon fills up with excreta and rotting uneaten food.

The pair does take it in turns to incubate the eggs, of which there are usually three, but the female always takes the night shift. The young hatch after 26–28 days, and on a very good day the adults may bring in a food item every five minutes. They grow quickly. It won't be long until they will need to migrate north.

WEEK 50

Harpy eagle

Harpia harpyja

CENTRAL AND SOUTH AMERICA
86–107cm (34–42in), WINGSPAN 1.8–2.2m (6–7¼ft)

 THE REPUTATION OF THE HARPY EAGLE is such that some professional bird tour companies organize trips with the sole purpose of trying to catch sight of it, undoubtedly the most formidable raptor in the world. It is the ultimate apex predator: very big, very powerful and very rare. Its talons are the size of a human fist and are the largest of any eagle, and the legs have a similar circumference to a child's wrist. The wingspan, not the greatest of any bird but close, can easily exceed 2m (6½ft). The enormous bill, which can be 6cm (2¼in) in length, tears the flesh off medium-sized mammals.

Nobody goes to listen to a harpy eagle singing or calling, though. Its penetrating, somewhat mournful whistles are feeble for such a large bird. And for most of the time it is quiet.

Throughout its wide range from Central America (especially Panama) and into the vast forests of Amazonia, the harpy eagle is extraordinarily difficult to see. Very few active kills have ever been witnessed. This is not a bird of prey that likes to soar high in the air or show itself above the canopy. Instead, it is highly secretive, remaining motionless on a single perch, often an elevated but hidden one, for hours on end. It catches some prey by slipping down from its lookout point and snatching it unawares from above.

The sheer power of the harpy eagle is indicated by the prey that it takes. Its main foods, as least measured by what it brings to the nest, are monkeys and sloths. Both of these groups live primarily in the trees and it is a curious fact that one group is supremely quick and agile, while the sloths are famous for being anything but, the latter presumably relying on camouflage to survive.

In common with most raptors, harpy eagles are opportunistic and at times simply catch what crosses their path.

The list of primates taken by harpy eagles is like a roll-call of all the Amazonian species, the largest being the howler monkeys (*Alouatta* spp.), which can reach 9kg (20lbs) in weight. Female harpy eagles are larger than males and are responsible for these spectacular kills, which are as heavy as the bird itself. The eagles will often haul the large corpses up to the top of a tree, away from any potential thieves. Most monkeys killed, though, are in the order of 1–4kg (2–9lbs) in weight, the latter still well above the range for most other raptors of the region. In at least one study, primates account for 37 per cent of the kills brought to a well-monitored nest.

The harpy eagles take a great toll on sloths, and they take all the species in a region. In a couple of studies similar to that mentioned above, sloths accounted for around 50 per cent of all kills recorded. One can imagine that it only takes the eagle to spot a sloth for the latter's fate to be sealed.

In common with most raptors, harpy eagles are opportunistic and at times simply catch what crosses their path. They are known to predate birds, especially larger ones such as macaws (see page 36) and curassows (Cracidae), and also a few reptiles. Other mammals caught have included tayras (*Eira barbara*), which are predatory themselves, and also more inoffensive animals such as porcupines and armadillos. In fact, almost anything of the right size can be on the radar of this formidable and majestic bird of prey.

Pairs of harpy eagles mate for life and make an enormous nest up to 1.2m (4ft) in diameter high up in an emergent tree, often a kapok (*Ceiba pentandra*) or a Brazil nut tree (*Bertholletia excelsa*). The female lays two eggs, of which normally only one hatches. The youngster is looked after for so long that each pair of harpies only produces one offspring every two years or so.

WEEK 51

Grey parrot

Psittacus erithacus

CENTRAL AFRICA

28–39cm (11–15½in)

PARROTS ARE EVERYONE'S IDEA OF tropical birds. And most people know that parrots squawk. However, if you listen to this recording of a wild grey parrot, you will be struck by the sheer variety of sounds that it makes. This is a perched bird high up in a mighty forest tree, just chatting away.

These sounds barely scratch the surface of this bird's extraordinary – and fabled – vocal abilities, which are now known the world over. It is the grey parrot's misfortune that its fame is greatest as a bird in captivity. But millennia ago, people realized that this bird could 'talk' – that is, it could imitate human speech very accurately, and they adopted it as a pet, first in the forests of Africa, then in Europe and beyond. Over its long history of domestication, however, what people never realized until very recently is that the grey parrot really can talk.

And it can count. And it can enjoy music. It can use tools. And make choices armed with complex information. Perhaps the world should be ruled by grey parrots. This extraordinary bird has many of the capabilities of a small child, and even a dash of empathy.

The grey parrot's ability to imitate is legendary. In the wild, it imitates the birds around it and also, apparently, the odd bat species. In human company, however, its learning ability becomes more obvious, and its vocabulary reflects what it hears. This has led to the odd headline, such as the group of grey parrots that had to be removed from a cage in a zoo because they kept on uttering profanities. There have even been a couple of cases where pet grey parrots were considered for use in a human prosecution trial. In 2017, one pet kept on repeating the phrase 'don't shoot', much to the chagrin of a wife accused of murdering her husband. However, it was not called to be a witness.

In the late 1970s, a young researcher named Dr Irene Pepperberg bought a grey parrot called Alex from a pet shop and began studying its cognitive abilities. The results, over many years, became more and more astonishing. Alex learned over 100 words and was also able to mash them together appropriately – such as saying 'yummy' plus 'bread' to refer to cake. He was able to respond to questions with correct answers about colour and texture, effectively conversing with his human companions, and forming simple sentences. He could recognize seven colours and five shapes. Once, looking in a mirror, he asked, 'What colour?' Shortly, he learned the word 'grey'. The ability of self-awareness, as confirmed by recognizing yourself in a mirror, is also a rare cognitive ability, mainly limited to apes.

Amazingly, Alex and other parrots showed the ability to count up to six (other parrots have now reached 17) and, still more impressively, to add numbers together, an attribute that was thought at the time to be limited to great apes. All in all, Pepperberg suggested that Alex could rival many of the abilities of a human toddler.

More and more studies are confirming these findings. One delightful one is that grey parrots have musical taste and favourite tunes. Using touch screens in their cages that play a wide variety of music, different parrots repeatedly play they ones that they like, different to their neighbours. Some have even been known to make requests to smart speakers! Had he been alive (he died in 2007), Alex might well have asked Alexa.

WEEK 52

Tinkling cisticola

Cisticola rufilatus

SOUTH-CENTRAL AFRICA

12–15cm (4¾–5in)

HAVE A LISTEN TO THIS RECORDING AND see what you think – can this sound be described as 'tinkling'? The dictionary defines tinkling as 'a light, clear ringing sound', so you can judge for yourself. To me, it sounds somewhat like a small tuneless bell being shaken at a rapid rate.

You might wonder why I am asking such a question. It's because, if you wish to immerse yourself in the vexed process of identifying cisticolas, you need to sharpen up your present participles. If you travel in Africa, you are going to come across a number of the following: singing, whistling, trilling, chattering – these are all genuine English names of different cisticolas. So are bubbling, rattling, churring, wailing, chirping, croaking and zitting cisticola. I promise you, this isn't a wind-up; and, by the way, there is a winding cisticola as well.

Some of these names are entirely apt. The zitting cisticola (*C. juncidis*) does indeed go 'zit-zit-zit ...' – endlessly as it happens. And the rattling cisticola (*C. chiniana*) absolutely makes a rattling sound. But the bubbling cisticola (*C. bulliens*)? Do me a favour. And so many birds trill and whistle that you would be hard put to declare their associated species the emphatic best in category.

You might wonder why any birds might have names like this, which come across, to be honest, as a joke from times past. But then you ask – what else could you call them? The cisticolas are a very large (around 50) group of small, streaky, often skulking birds with no sense that they need to be exciting and colourful. Usually, identifying them, at least in the field, comes down to voice. You cannot call all of them 'streaky cisticola'. And, let's be honest, it's good publicity. The entertaining names have made some very niche birds much better known than they otherwise would have been. Happily, the names in other languages often follow suit. For example, the French name for whistling cisticola (*C. lateralis*) is *cisticole siffleuse* and that for singing cisticola (*C. cantans*) is *cisticole chanteuse*.

We need to give grateful thanks to a certain Hubert Lynes for giving the cisticolas any love at all. Back in the 1920s he devoted months to three African expeditions, each with the sole aim of collecting cisticolas and sorting them out. His devotion to being a nerd does him a credit that resounds down the ages. From an original 200 suggested species, he rationalized this down to the number it is now.

And what of the name 'cisticola'? This comes from two Latin words, in reverse order: *colo*, meaning 'I inhabit', and *cista*, meaning 'basket'. The name refers to the cisticolas' unusual nests, which are often closely woven structures with a spherical or bottle shape. In the case of the subject of this entry, the tinkling cisticola, the nest is ball-like with a side entrance at the top, made up of grass stems. It has a dishevelled appearance, presumably intentionally to avoid standing out, and is placed very low down in a grass tussock, with which it is often interwoven.

This is a widespread but poorly known cisticola. It is very shy and difficult to see, remaining hidden in its favourite long grass. It keeps very low and, if necessary, it can hop across the ground to escape unwanted attention. The few observations suggest that it is usually found in groups of 4–5, presumably consisting of adults and their latest brood of young.

But in the breeding season at least, it does tinkle.

Index

African fish eagle 31
Andean cock-of-the-rock 164–7
antbird, ocellated 16–19
Aristotle 106
Asian koel 104–7
Attenborough, Davd 101–2
azure-winged magpie 90

babbler, jungle 9, 184–7
bay wren 11, 152–5
bee-eaters 72–5, 114
bee hummingbird 25
bellbird, white 57
Bible 118
biodiversity 7–8
birds-of-paradise 8, 40–3, 101, 176–9
black-collared lovebird 134
black drongo 90
black-faced solitaire 60–3
black-naped oriole 124–7
black-winged lovebird 134
blue-and-yellow macaw 36–9
blue whistling thrush 96–9
bluish-fronted jacamar 112–15
bowerbird, golden 148–51
breeding, communal 9, 46–7, 54, 185–7
brown shrike 90
brown wood-owl 64–7
buff-breasted paradise

kingfisher 204–7
buffalo-weaver, white-headed 54, 55
bulbul, yellow-vented 172–5
bush-shrikes 146
bustard, kori 74

calls/call notes 10
cisticola, tinkling 216–19
climate change 15
cock-of-the-rock, Andean 164–7
colour 9, 22–3, 27, 51, 71
cordonbleu, red-cheeked 160–3
cotinga 8, 57
courtship see mating behaviour
cranes 74
crow, house 106, 128–31
cuckoos 88–91, 106
curassows 211

dark-necked tailorbird 120–3
dodo 35
drongos 90, 127
duetting 11, 145–7, 153–4, 157, 190
Dumbacher, Jack 102, 103

eagles 31, 208–11
eastern paradise whydah 92–5
echolocation 85–6
eggs, number of 9
Emperor penguins 15

fairywren, purple-crowned 9, 76–9
feather sounds 47, 157–8
fiery-throated hummingbird 24–7
finches 94, 137
fire-tailed sunbird 68–71
flamingo, lesser 28–31
fledging 9
fruit-dove, wompoo 196–9

Galápagos penguin 12–15
golden bowerbird 148–51
gonolek, yellow-crowned 11, 144–7
goose, spur-winged 103
greater-bird-of-paradise 176–9
green-winged pytilia 94
greenbul, joyful 174
grey parrot 212–15
Guianan cock-of-the-rock 165

harpy eagle 208–11
Hawaiian honeycreepers 137–9
honeyeaters 67
hooded pitohui 100–3
hornbill, rhinoceros 156–9
house crow 106, 128–31
Humboldt penguin 14
hummingbirds 24–7, 140–3

ʻIʻiwi 136–9

Indian cuckoo 88–91
Indian peafowl 116–19
iridescence 27, 50

jacamar, bluish-fronted 112–15
Jackson, Michael 45
Jones, Carl 34
joyful greenbul 174
jungle babbler 9, 184–7

king of saxony bird-of-paradise 40–3
kingfisher, buff-breasted paradise 204–7
koel, Asian 104–7
kookaburra 205
kori bustard 74
Kricher, John 58–9

laughing kookaburra 205
laughingthrushes 106
leks 9, 46–7, 59, 165–7
lifespans 9, 10, 151
long-tailed tit 185
lovebird, red-headed 132–5
Lynes, Hubert 218

macaques, crab-eating 34
macaws 36–9, 211
Malayan banded pitta 108–11
manakins 8, 44–7
marabou stork 31
mating behaviour
  display 8–9, 42–3, 46–7, 51, 94–5, 118–19, 151, 178–9
leks 9, 46–7, 59, 165–7
pair bonds 9–10, 11, 211
melba finch 94
migration 206
mimicry 93–4, 115, 190, 214
monkeys 53–4
Moreau, Reginald Ernst 174
Müllerian mimicry 115
music inspiration 174
mynas 106, 168–71

nests
bay wren 154–5
black-faced solitaire 63
black-naped oriole 126–7
blue whistling thrush 99
buff-breasted paradise kingfisher 207
common potoo 203
dark-necked tailorbird 122–3
fire-tailed sunbird 71
hooded pitohui 103
house crow 130
lesser flamingo 31
red-cheeked cordonbleu 162–3
red-headed lovebird 134–5
rhinoceros hornbill 159
screaming piha 58
superb starling 54, 55
tinkling cisticola 218–19
village weaver 181–3
white-browed robin-chat 191
wompoo fruit-dove 198
nightingales 174
nightjars 86, 202
nocturnal birds 64–7, 84–7, 201–3
northern carmine bee-eater 72–5

ocellated antbird 16–19
oilbird 84–7
orioles 10, 124–7
ostrich 74
owls 64–7
oxpeckers 80–3

pair bonds 9–10, 11, 211
parasite birds 88–95, 106–7
parrot, grey 212–15
peafowl, Indian 116–19
penguin, Galápagos 12–15
Pepperberg, Irene 214–15
pigeons 32–5, 196–9
piha, screaming 56–9
pink pigeon 32–5
pitohui, hooded 100–3
pitta, Malayan banded 108–11
poison 102–3
potoo, common 200–3
purple-crested turaco 20–3
purple-crowned fairywren 9, 76–9
pytilia, green-winged 94

quetzal, resplendent 48–51

rhinoceros hornbill 156–9
robin-chat, white-browed 188–91

screaming piha 56–9
secretarybird 74
shrikes 90, 106, 146
Slud, Paul 62
solitaire, black-faced 60–3
songs
  definition 10
  duets 11, 145–7, 153–4, 157, 190
  females 10
  mimicry 93–4, 190, 214
southern carmine bee-eater 74
sparkling violetear 140–3
splendid fairywren 77
spur-winged goose 103
starling, superb 9, 52–5
storks 31, 74
streak-backed oriole 10
sunbirds 26, 68–71
superb fairywren 77, 79
superb starling 9, 52–5
swiftlets 86

tailorbird, dark-necked 120–3
thrushes 61, 96–9, 191
tinkling cisticola 216–19
toco toucan 192–5
tropics, defined 7, 9
turaco, purple-crested 20–3

Vedas 106
village weaver 180–3
violetear, sparkling 140–3
vocalisation generally 10

waxbills 162
weavers 54, 55, 162–3, 180–3
white bellbird 57
white-browed robin-chat 188–91
white-headed buffalo-weaver 54, 55
whydahs 92–5, 163
wing-snapping 47
wompoo fruit-dove 196–9

Acknowledgements

I would like to thank Madeleine Floyd for her wonderful artistic and beautiful illustrations, which absolutely lighten up this book and are probably responsible for most of our potential royalties! Crucial also are the many recordists, mentioned at the back of the book, who have ventured into all those tropical places and made the effort to record the birds! I would like to thank those at Batsford for their help, especially long-suffering Nicola Newman who has been the most fabulous support, as well as Lilly Phelan, Magda Simoes-Brown and Katie Hewitt. My family, namely my wife Carolyn and children Emmie and Sam, I am grateful for being by my side.

Also, several people have facilitated some wonderful trips to tropical regions which has provided inspiration for the text. These include, among many, Serge Arias in Costa Rica, Katinka Domen in Honduras and Herbert Byaruhanga in Uganda, as well as the Tourist Boards of those countries, plus Sabah and Brunei.

We would like to thank xeno-canto (xeno-canto.org) for providing an open platform for sharing sound recordings of nature, and the following recordists for their contribution:

Andrew Spencer (XC71520, XC17240, XC209990, XC547543), Bram Piot (XC856163, XC405791), David Boyle (XC921805), Eloisa Matheu (XC582833), Eric Seidlitz (XC477488), Frank Lambert (XC517652, XC429496, XC429956, XC409047, XC409194, XC501293, XC771974), Gabriel Leite (XC597717, XC730949, XC891625), Geoff Carey (XC879327), Hans Matheve (XC155388, XC699831), Jesse Fagan (XC383122), John V. Moore (XC279297), Kent Livezey (XC661034), Luiz C. Silva (XC601401), Neils Krabbe (XC785828, XC343734), Patrik Åberg (XC97335, XC98593, XC96923, XC401354),

Peter Boesman (XC271495, XC271507, XC271392, XC426369, XC300471, XC223278, XC739368, XC719234, XC739609, XC223872), Richard E. Webster (XC705946, XC708796), Sandra V. Valderrama (XC126445), Scott Connop (XC594572), Simon Elliott (XC590464, XC594950, XC840504, XC113090, XC590868), Viral Joshi (XC794970).

All recordings included in this book can be heard at www.batsfordbooks.com/a-year-of-tropical-birdsong/ and xeno-canto.org

Further reading

Birds of the World (Cornell Lab of Ornithology) – birdsoftheworld.org

Cocker, M. *Birds and People*. Jonathan Cape.

Bartley, G and Swash, A. *Hummingbirds*. Princeton University Press.

Frith, CB and Beehler, BM. *The Birds of Paradise*. OUP.

Kirwan, G and Green, G. *Cotingas and Manakins*. Christopher Helm.

Kricher, J. *The New Neotropical Companion*. Princeton University Press.

Sibley, D et al. *The Sibley Guide to Bird Life and Behaviour*. Christopher Helm.

Handbook of the Birds of the World, volumes 1-16. Lynx Edicions, Barcelona.

The Birds of Africa, volumes 1-7. Christopher Helm/Academic Press.

Handbook of Australian, New Zealand and Antarctic Birds, volumes 1-7. OUP.

Batsford is committed to respecting the intellectual property rights of others. We have taken all reasonable efforts to ensure that the reproduction of all contents on these pages is done with the full consent of the copyright owners. If you are aware of unintentional omissions, please contact the company directly so that any necessary correction may be made for future editions.